THE LEADERSHIP ESSENTIALS

A Practical Handbook for Success

Workplace Series Presentation

Partha Pratim Pal

Dr. Jones Mathew

First Published in April 2020

ISBN: 978-93-90034-52-9

Price: INR 250/-

BLUEROSE PUBLISHERS
www.bluerosepublishers.com
info@bluerosepublishers.com
+91 8882 898 898

Cover Design:
Tyngshain Pariat

Typographic Design:
Tanya Raj Upadhyay

Distributed by: BlueRose, Amazon, Flipkart, Shopclues

Acknowledgment

This work would not have been possible if the authors had not had the opportunity to experience and observe the numerous leadership issues during their long corporate and academic journeys. The leaders who went before exhibited some good and some not so good qualities and flaws. Each was a learning experience. This book is dedicated to all those leaders who we learnt from - whether it be the traits to acquire or the failures to be wary of.

Our parents must receive all the credit for whatever we have accomplished and for the blessings to put it all into a structured work such as this one. Without them we would be nothing.

Gratitude is due to our families for providing their support silently and often unknowingly while we worked long hours in our studios writing this book.

Many thanks to Blue Rose Publishing for the exhaustive reviews of the manuscript time and again and coaxing us to complete the work within a reasonable amount of time.

Finally, thanks to all the aspiring managers who dream of becoming effective and unique leaders. Without their hunger to improve themselves, this book would not have the same intensity of purpose.

Partha Pratim Pal, Bangalore

Jones Mathew,PhD, New Delhi

January 2020

Prologue

I hear and I forget

I see and I remember

I do and I understand

(Confucius: 551–479 BC)

Leadership has been one of the most discussed, debated and written subjects by academicians, professionals, authors and journalists over many past decades.

Why is leadership such an important subject?

It has been well established that the quality of leaders, both good and otherwise, has a bearing on the quality of life of those who are associated with them.

A good leader creates an ecosystem which affects the life of the team members in an organization; or the life of its citizens when it comes to a state or country not only of its present generations but also of future generations.

A pertinent definition from Field Marshal Sir Bill Slim may be stated here: 'There is a difference between leadership and management. Leadership is of the spirit, compounded of personality and vision; its practice is an art. Management is of the mind, a matter of accurate calculation… Its practice is a science. Managers are necessary; leaders are essential.'

He also goes on to say, 'Leaders are made more often than they are born. You all have leadership in you. Develop it by thought training and by practice.'

The essence of this workbook is based on the Confucian philosophy — I do and I understand.

There are many definitions of leadership but one that we feel is most appropriate for leadership in business is this:

Leadership in business is the ability of a company's management to make sound decisions, and develop and inspire their team to perform.

Broadly:

- ✓ Leadership is about results.
- ✓ Leadership ensures that people achieve greater results than they thought were possible for them to achieve.
- ✓ Leadership enables the team to upgrade their skills, learn to collaborate with multiple functions and team members, and most importantly, in the process, enjoy their work in particular and life in general.
- ✓ Leadership inspires people to look at the bigger picture and focus their energy and efforts in achieving the organizational vision.

According to Keith Davis, "Leadership is the ability to persuade others to seek defined objectives enthusiastically. It is the human factor which binds a group together and motivates it towards goals."

This workbook was born out of the realization that leadership lessons are lost as young managers are not able to practice what they learn. In the rush of daily firefighting, there are fewer opportunities to put into practice the lessons acquired by observing, learning and absorbing from other leaders.

You would agree that there is no better learning methodology than experience which is practical and hands-on.

As implementation is undertaken, the young manager gets a mixture of both: desired results and crushing disappointments. Sometimes the outcomes are as per expectations, at other times not. There is often confusion why the leadership style that worked for other leaders does not work now. There are many reasons for that anomaly. What works for some, may not work for others.

This workbook is an endeavour to assist young managers understand themselves and practice their learnings as they go along. In-depth introspection, deliberation, and understanding of their personal leadership style will be employed to examine what has worked (or not) for them till now and what needs to be done in the future to become more effective leaders. The carefully crafted chapters will take the reader through a logical flow of steps to attain excellent leadership qualities. We advise that the aspiring leader proceed chapter wise in order to obtain the maximum advantage from this workbook. Though each chapter is linked to the next, the reader can benefit from going back and forth to a chapter of his or her choice to absorb material that is of immediate relevance.

This workbook is divided into three modules.

Module- I

- Leading with Integrity and Honesty: A leader must stand up for what is "right". Integrity is about character, avoiding moral shortcuts and fostering long term success. It teaches how you can build leadership based on integrity and honesty for the team to follow.

- Self-Awareness: How to make the best use of your emotions for the team to benefit from your presence. Successful leaders know where their natural inclinations lie and use this knowledge to boost those inclinations or compensate for them.

- Servant Leadership: Servant leadership is primarily about giving priority to team members' needs, helping them to grow as persons and in their profession. This is the essence of servant leadership. You will also come to appreciate why the servant leadership style is in demand today.

Module- II

- Vision of a Leader: Leading is about going somewhere by having clear goals and implementing initiatives. SMART goal setting and creating an energizing vision for the team are key to leadership success.

- Courage, Confidence, Conviction and Commitment: Leadership is about demonstrating and inculcating these four qualities or traits in the team.

- Communication: Words have energy and it is important to know how to use them properly. It includes tone of voice, body language in communication and the power of listening.

Module- III

- How to handle failure: Leadership involves developing resilience in adverse situations, keeping the team upbeat when faced with failure, being with the team when things don't go as expected and using failures as stepping stones to future success.

- Celebrating success: Leadership requires one to be a successful creator and a successful finder. High quality leaders appreciate the importance of positive strokes. Teams come together to achieve majestic accomplishments when their smaller achievements get appreciated.

- Innovation: This is the lifeblood of any organization today. Leaders must have mastery over the mechanics of innovation, the ability to create the ecosystem necessary to foster innovation, and effectively measure and map innovative behaviour.

- Situation Leadership: This is of the essence to the achievement of an effective leadership track record. One size fits all is a common mistake leaders make. Trying to make a large number of employees adapt to *your* leadership style may not always be the best strategy. What if you could adjust to *their* skills and commitment levels?

Why should anyone be led by you? What would make you an unstoppable leader? The above modules are designed to make you the leader that you aspire to be. Great leaders are the need of the hour. We hope this workbook helps you to fill that void.

After mastering the Leadership Essentials workbook, we hope you will join us for the *Spartacus Leadership Development Program* (SLDP), where we facilitate the participants to go on a leadership discovery journey with the help of one-on-one coaching, making our leader outcomes a tribute to the legendary Thracian gladiator warrior-leader of the first century BCE, Spartacus, who gave the mighty Romans some serious thoughts about their invincibility.

Your feedback is most welcome and we look forward to receiving your thoughts on improving this workbook for future readers.

Let's walk together on this effective leadership development journey. Good Luck! Benediximus! Happy Leading!

Partha Pratim Pal, Bangalore, India.

Jones Mathew, PhD., New Delhi, India.

January 2020

CONTENTS

LEADERSHIP ESSENTIAL # 1
INTEGRITY

Integrity is the practice of being honest and showing consistent and uncompromising adherence to strong moral and ethical principles and values. In ethics, integrity is regarded as honesty and truthfulness of one's actions. Integrity is the opposite of hypocrisy and dishonesty.

Why do we begin with integrity as an important leadership essential? The answer is simple enough: without integrity, one has no moral right to lead.

Why is integrity important in leadership? Simply because it is the cornerstone of the ability to persuade people you lead on a long term basis. Also because it beats power-through-position hands down any day.

Possessing and displaying integrity in the workplace is one of the most important qualities of great leadership in business.

> *"The supreme quality for leadership is unquestionably integrity. Without it, no real success is possible, no matter whether it is on a section gang, a football field, in an army, or in an office."*
>
> *Dwight D. Eisenhower, 34th President of the United States*

Let's examine why.

Integrity is the ability and willingness to tell the truth as it is, irrespective of its cost to oneself. Integrity demands standing up for something when it is seen to be the call of the hour. A leader must stand up for what is "right".

Integrity is about character. It is about never taking moral shortcuts. Integrity helps in being successful over the long term.

A high integrity individual refuses to compromise on good principles. Business situations often throw up opportunities to do the "easy but wrong thing". Integrity is your shield. One cannot have integrity without strong moral and ethical grounding.

Integrity is an all-inclusive character quality. It is not possible to have integrity in one domain and not in others. One cannot have integrity in accounting practices and not have it in business development. A leader cannot have integrity while dealing with suppliers while being immoral with opposite gender employees.

Integrity is a binary construct. It is either a zero or a one. A leader either has it or not. There are no grey areas when it comes to integrity. Therefore, leaders must begin by communicating and displaying a clear compass of integrity. The true North is clear and the needle never wavers. Team members know exactly what to expect and deliver. They can count on a leader with integrity to do the right thing. Always. What an assurance! No ambiguity. No confusion. No chance of misinterpretation. Impact on business success can only be phenomenal.

A leader with integrity is one who demonstrates honesty and dependability.

A leader establishes honesty and dependability through years of demonstrated behaviours. Promises are kept every time.

The leader must walk the talk, even when the odds are not favourable.

In case of inability to do what was promised, the leader apologises and explains why the promise could not be honoured.

Transparency in dealings with the team is a hallmark of such a leader.

Ann Mulcahy, the former CEO of Xerox Corporation, was a candid leader. Soon after she took over Xerox, she pronounced its business model unsustainable, and that the company would have to confront reality and make tough decisions to return to profitability. Because of her integrity, she gained the trust of the employees, who then pulled together, gave their best efforts and brought Xerox back into the black.

Such a leader may not profusely praise team members in a one-on-one discussion but would be a strong defender of the team in front of superiors. Straight talking, saying what one means and meaning what one says is such a leader's natural characteristics.

Though one may not like the bluntness, the team members know that whatever their leader does, it is for the benefit of the entire team.

Cutting corners or bending rules are non-options when business issues are discussed. Such leaders teach the team to be well within the normative boundaries of the organization and yet win, year after year.

Leaders with integrity find opportunities to be different and not follow the herd unless it is aligned with personal and professional values.

Progress may be slow in the beginning, but the team discovers its new capabilities, not known to them till now, giving them more self-confidence as they find a new purpose in their professional lives.

> "The greatness of a man is not in how much wealth he acquires, but in his integrity and his ability to affect those around him positively."
>
> Bob Marley, Jamaican pioneer of Reggae Music

The team under leaders with integrity realise they can do much more than they thought they could by flowing with the crowd; their leader's thinking process is different — an individual with integrity who will not compromise. Team members get that.

If a leader breaks or bends the rules of the organization or any other law or encourages or forces his team members to do the same, then they are in violation of the sacred covenant of integrity that they are expected to uphold. Such leaders corrupt their subordinates. This corruption not only occurs at the business activity or functional level but also at the moral and ethical level of subordinates. This then expands into the industry and national level. In short, a leader with low integrity can create a pool of low integrity subordinates who then go on to become low integrity business leaders. Imagine the negative impact on a nation with a large number of low integrity business leaders!

Financial integrity is paramount in any leadership role.

Dishonest people despite knowing that they should not indulge in financial irregularities, cannot control the urge to make quick gains.

Some may make personal gains by successfully indulging in unscrupulous financial activities, which over time make them quite confident of their devious craft, turning it into a habit. Often it becomes a part of their extra income and then the habit becomes a compulsion to support an extravagant lifestyle riding on unethical financial gains. Ultimately, when their financial misdemeanours are brought to light, they not only lose their jobs but also become untouchables in the industry. Disaster strikes their personal lives, as their family suffers financially and also socially.

Financial illegalities do not happen without connivance of or tacit approval from important people in the hierarchy, most notably the immediate manager. Good leaders do not allow anyone within the organization to take undue advantage of their positions to sabotage the organization's reputation.

Integrity is more difficult than it seems. A few reasons for this are:

1. People's ability to rationalize anything makes it possible for them to say that *it's not really cheating* or *everybody else does it too*.
2. Different people define integrity differently – some cultures encourage gifting (Diwali in India) while others would consider it as bribing.

When you sit across from a client do you tweak facts to suit your company? Are promises made that are not intended to be honoured? Are mistakes owned up to? These are important questions a leader must answer. Integrity is doing the "right" thing even when no one is watching. Again, defining "right" is also not easy. The culture in which the business is embedded determines "right" and "wrong" for most leaders. To stand up for the truth and be a 'minority of one' is the true test of a leader with integrity.

Exercise:

You have planned to attend a family wedding two months from now in another city. You take your immediate manager into confidence and then plan an official tour on the same dates as that of the marriage. You may extend a day or two and take leave for the same. Would this be high integrity behaviour? Yes or No? _________

Has the manager lived up to his responsibility as the custodian of integrity and honesty in his team: Yes or No?

____

____

Is the above an issue of financial integrity: Yes or No? Why do you think so?

____

____

____

Unfortunately, some of these people also move up in their career, and they bank on their dishonesty to indulge in bigger 'deals'.

There are many once-illustrious names in various industries all around the world who have compromised integrity and ended up in jail. Most such people tend to be over-confident of being able to fool the system and survive unscathed. Time and again this has been proved wrong. Time and again the law has shown it possesses very long arms.

There should be no exceptions to honesty and integrity. Integrity is a state of mind and is not situational. Integrity is a philosophy of life. If you compromise your integrity in small situations with little consequences, then it paves the way for compromises on bigger situations with far-reaching consequences.

Leaders with integrity always err on the side of fairness, especially when other people are unfair.

It is human to have a personal liking for some team members over the others, but a good leader is conscious of the fact that all team members deserve fairness in all forms and his every action is a demonstration of his fairness.

When a leader treats any person unfairly or does not support him in bad times, he must understand that his action is being watched by the team members. It spreads negativity in the team, and quite naturally other team members know what is in store for them in the future in similar situations. Being with your team members in bad times or when things are not going well for them is a sign of concern and warmth. Team members respect that. Only honest leaders can do this credibly.

Everyone can be good to his team members when the sales and marketing figures are rosy, but it takes the character of a good leader to support and encourage team members during rough patches.

And life is a cycle of good and bad patches, so abandoning team members in bad times will result in the team abandoning the leader in good times.

Being fair to every team member is the hallmark of a leader with high integrity.

You would have realized by now that integrity is demonstrated as honesty and dependability, fairness and transparency.

When a leader is consistent in demonstrating honesty and dependability over and over again in various testing situations, he gains the respect and trust of his team members.

Trust is the only currency of a leader in today's work environment.

The team will go more than an extra mile for a leader they trust.

Team members will forgo short term gains and even undergo hardships if they trust their leader.

Leaders who enjoy the trust of their team members will make the workplace more productive, enjoyable and in such teams, a conflict is a rare event.

In today's cluttered market place, with very little or no product/service differentiation, a vibrant and cohesive team is about the only serious differentiator.

Such teams can only be created and developed by leaders who enjoy the trust of their team members.

Hence, trust is the most valuable currency of a leader which is possible only if the leader demonstrates high honesty and integrity.

Integrity is also about giving and keeping promises diligently. In today's times to be a leader with integrity requires guts of steel. Short term gains through shortcuts have become so prevalent that for a person of integrity to hold his ground has become exceedingly difficult. Integrity is not for the weak-hearted. It is not useful if one wants to be the most popular person in the organization. In fact, people with high integrity are often sabotaged with false allegations and character assassination. Hence, integrity requires strong nerves.

Can integrity be developed?

Without a doubt, yes.

Exercise:

A high performing salesman is accused of sexually harassing a female subordinate and the leader ignores it in light of the phenomenal hold on the market the sales man has; firing him might result in the company losing major clients and market share. Is he a good leader? Yes or No. Why?

____

____

____

____

____

Exercise:

As a leader you are to choose between a high performer who is not very friendly with you (does not go on socializing sessions with you outside of work) and a moderate performer (who spends a lot of time socializing with you outside of work and is a good friend to you) for promotion. Who would you select? Why?

____

____

____

____

____

Integrity requires sacrifices to be made. Monetary benefits, comforts and convenience, belongingness, shortcuts, disproportionately high standards of living and popularity are some sacrifices to be made.

The reward for integrity in business leadership is, becoming a "legend". Added benefits are a head held high, life-long loyalty from similarly minded team members, peace of mind, and long term success.

Vignette # 1

Rajeev's team missed a deadline for an important deliverable his team was supposed to have developed and delivered. He took responsibility for the missed deadline even though his team hadn't delivered as promised. He discussed the problems with his team and they put in place precautions, checks and balances that would prevent them from underperforming again.

Team members realized their part in the failure but the consequences were controlled because Rajeev took responsibility as the team lead. We believe Rajeev was a leader with integrity.

Vignette # 2

Shalini was the HR Manager for a major telecom company. A female employee approached her to complain against her male boss who was bullying her. Shalini as the HR Head took charge and investigated the complaint and found it to be true. Other employees too had been bullied in the same manner by that boss. She offered to mediate a conversation between the boss and the employee. The employee was scared to confront her boss directly. Nevertheless, Shalini gave her assurance. The boss blamed the employee for shoddy work. Ultimately, Shalini had to escalate the matter to the Senior VP level who was the boss of the accused. Only then did that person desist from his obnoxious behavior. This is an example of high integrity leadership on the part of the HR Head.

Now the pertinent question is: how to build 'trust' among team members?

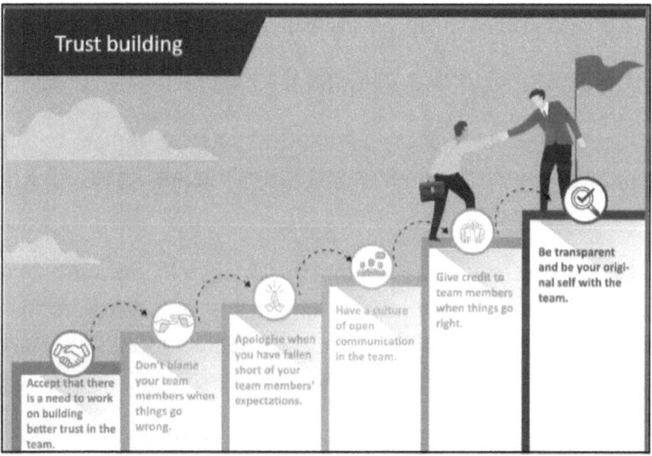

Trust is the culture of an organization that has to start at the top. It is a leadership responsibility. It flows from integrity. Hence this next section delves into the trust building aspect which is best witnessed in organizations with a high integrity leadership quotient.

Any company that is having trouble is a company that has an issue of trust deficit between the team and its leader.

When there is a trust deficit, the environment is filled with fear.

Fear in the workplace is the most damaging of emotions which spirals the organization downwards with enormous speed.

The environment becomes toxic which causes conflicts, poor performance, employee attrition, low commitment and bad-mouthing of the company in the job market.

It is only natural that such an environment does not attract talent; on the contrary, it will repel talent.

An organization that is low on the trust factor will decay.

Hence, developing an environment of trust should be the paramount responsibility of a leader at all levels, and it needs to start from the top.

Leaders recruit team members taking into account their competencies, their past achievements and track record, assessing their job fit and their aspirations to make a mark in their careers in the company.

They come to work with loads of aspirations and expect support and encouragement to do their job to meet their assigned goals so that they are professionally successful.

What makes them good or bad at their work is indeed the culture of the organization.

Let's discuss some ways on how to build trust in the team and hence the culture of trust in the organization.

1. **<u>Be willing to accept that there is a need to work on building better trust in the team.</u>**

Any management will be open to improving physical objects without much problem.

If an employee informs his leader that there is a problem with the office wifi or that the IT system does not have enough bandwidth, the leader would have no problem admitting that it needs to be upgraded or changed.

However, when it comes to organizational culture, it is a different ball game altogether. It is difficult to admit that there is a need to make changes in the culture of the organization or the team.

Willing to make the change exhibits the courage and character of the leader, and this is the first step towards gaining trust from team members.

There are various tools to understand the level of employee trust levels.

Employee engagement surveys are one way to understand various aspects or parameters on how the company is functioning including the trust level of various teams.

HR departments often organize the leader's orientation programs or 360° feedback mechanisms to understand the trust levels between the leader and team members.

Exercise:

Do you recognize that there needs to be a change in the culture of your team? Why?

____

____

____

____

What are the cultural changes you want to bring about in your team?

____

____

____

____

What will you do to bring about the above changes?

____

____

____

____

2. <u>Don't blame your team members when things go wrong.</u>

Make every task a team effort and define roles and responsibilities. When team members are clear about their goals and they have the tools and training to work on achieving their goals, then people are more focused and usually do a good job.

In case one is not up to the mark, it is better to discuss and understand what the problem is and together form an action plan to solve it by supporting each other.

This behaviour of the leader will give a sense amongst the team that "we are in it together" and "we win or lose as a team".

Being involved as an insider rather than worrying about an external threat brings more ownership amongst the team members and gradually members go the extra mile to accomplish the task.

STEPS TO INTEGRITY-BASED, TRUST DRIVEN TEAMS

Step 1: Tell the team it is a "Team"

Step 2: Define roles and responsibilities with high integrity

Step 3: Train members to trust and work together

Step 4: Discuss and understand why low performance is happening

Step 5: Praise good performance fairly

Step 6: Work as a Team on action plans

Overarching step: Be transparent, fair, display honesty and integrity throughout, and communicate regularly.

Exercise:

In your opinion is there someone who is pulling down your team's performance? Why do you think so?

____

____

____

____

Have you ever given honest feedback to this person privately or in a review meeting for the low performance?

Yes/No

How well did he know his roles? Not at all/ Fairly well/Completely?

Did you empower him with the right tools and training? Yes/No?

In the last 6 months how many times have you communicated with him on an individual basis? <5/>5

What was the outcome of these communications?

____

____

____

____

____

____

If you did provide feedback publicly or in person, did the employee's performance show any signs of improvement?

Yes/No

What are the areas which need improvement for better performance?

____

____

____

____

____

____

How do you plan to help the team member to improve?

____

____

____

____

____

3. <u>Apologise when you have fallen short of your team members' expectations.</u>

Leaders are human too and make mistakes, small or big, and some are big enough to pull down the performance of the team.

Admitting one's mistakes attracts admiration as a leader and signals that this is an honest person who does not use his position to cover up mistakes.

Such honest behaviour develops mutual trust and bonds the team together.

Exercise:

List the mistakes related to integrity that you as a leader have done in the last three months.

____
____
____
____
____
____

Which mistake(s) affected the performance of your team the most?

____
____
____
____
____

How would you have reacted if any of the team members committed similar mistakes?

____

____

____

____

____

____

Let's practice how to apologize to the team members for your mistakes.

"Hello everybody. I am here to apologise to each one of you for the leadership shortfall on my part. The entire team has been under tremendous pressure for the shortfall in our sales achievement. I do believe that our sales projections did not go as planned. My analysis is that I should have been more careful about the seasonality factor in the demand for our product. Nevertheless, lesson learned. Going forward I intend to look into every possible scenario so that we do not end up missing our targets. I must take the blame for this fiasco. I am sure we can regroup and re-emerge as the most successful team in the upcoming festive season by overachieving our October targets by 20%. This will help offset the current situation and bring glory back to our team! Are we all in?! Thank you."

4. <u>Have a culture of open communication in the team</u>

Leaders who depend more on one-to-one communication amongst the team members develop a culture of openness and direct feedback with their team.

Mails and other official memos should be kept to the minimum, so that communication is more one-to-one or in a group setting, for the team to express their views on what is going to propel the team forward.

In such an environment, the team accepts "s t r e t c h" goals and makes action plans to make those goals happen.

A trustworthy leader can create such openness and team members rise to the occasion to face challenges.

Exercise:

According to you, when and what matter(s) should you communicate over mail to your team?

____

____

____

____

____

____

____

Please give an example of the mail.

____

____

____

____

____

____

____

What is the general format of your team's meetings?

____

Let's do a one-on-one discussion on a performance review with a team member.
What are the key issues to be discussed?

____

What do you want to achieve through this discussion?

____

5. <u>Give credit to team members when things go right.</u>

Leaders who are confident of themselves, shower praise on their team members and give them the credit when they achieve organizational objectives.

Such behaviour by the leader builds trust amongst the team members and they get up on stage and sincerely thank their leader for having contributed to their success.

Leaders with integrity present team members to the top management and praise them in front of the top brass. Such leaders find ways to highlight their good work amongst all in the organization.

Such behaviour by the leader makes him stand out taller than any other leader who craves attention and credit, and their team members are prepared to give more than is required to see the team on top.

<u>Exercise:</u>
Give some examples when you have praised a team member in public for a good job done.

____

____

____

____

____

____

____

Did you let top management know about his or her success?

Yes/No

If yes, then what did you tell the top management of their achievement?

____

____

____

____

____

____

____

6. <u>Be transparent and be your original self with the team.</u>

People gauge their leader in his every word and action. The best way to build trust in the team is to be your own self. Fakes are recognized faster than one realizes and having a hidden agenda or pep talks for short term gains are a definite no-no if one has to build a team on trust and mutual respect.

In case the leader is up against some odds, it is better to share with the team and find a way out. This will offer a new purpose for the team to stick together to fight new battles as one formidable force.

Please recall if you have been tempted to give pep talks for short term gains which may not have been entirely true?

____

____

____

____

____

____

____

How can one be one's own self in front of the team?

____

____

____

____

____

____

____

Key learnings from this chapter for you:

1.

2.

3.

4.

In ancient India, Emperor Chandragupta Maurya (reign: c. 321 – c. 297 BCE), the founder of the Mauryan Empire had a Chief Minister by the name of Chanakya (also known as Kautilya). He was the author of the ancient Indian political treatise, the *Arthashastra*, which is still considered a seminal work in the field of political science and economics in India.

The fame and name of Chanakya spread far and wide so much so that once a Chinese visitor came to Pataliputra looking for Chanakya. On not finding Chanakya in the King's palace, he looked elsewhere and found him on the outskirts of the city, in a small hut in a remote place. The Chinese visitor was impressed by the wisdom and humility of Pataliputra's ruler. "When the minister stays in a simple dwelling, the subjects enjoy good housing; when the minister lavishes on his stay, then the subjects will be bereft of decent dwelling places."

One of the most important qualities of a minister is being, "swachh." Swachh is not simply being externally clean, but also indicates integrity and transparency, which is illustrated in the story below.

When a Chinese traveller entered the hut, it was dark and only a small oil lamp was burning inside. Chanakya welcomed the traveller inside and then lit another lamp and put out the flame of the first lamp.

The Chinese traveller was confused and didn't understand why another lamp was lit and the earlier one was put out upon his entry. "Is this lighting of a new lamp a tradition to welcome someone to the house?" he wondered aloud.

Chanakya smiled and answered quietly, "When you came in, I was doing the King's work, and the oil for that lamp was paid for by the king. Whenever I do my personal work, I light the other lamp, and the oil for this lamp is paid for by me, from my personal funds. Now that I am talking to you, I will be doing my personal work and not the King's work, and therefore, I will be using my own money to light the new lamp."

This is an excellent example of integrity, which is not only about external cleansing, but a total synergy between thoughts, words, and action.

This is a fundamental learning about the basics of integrity and character, without which a leader cannot get the trust of his team members.

Integrity is a binary construct.
It is Zero or One; Black or White; No Greys.

What one does when no one is looking

Telling the truth no matter how tough the consequences.

Standing up for what is right

- Refusal to compromise on good principles.

- Demonstrating honesty & dependability, fairness &transparency.

LEADERSHIP ESSENTIAL # 2
SELF AWARENESS

Self-awareness *is the capacity for introspection and the ability to recognize oneself as an individual separate from the environment and other individuals.*

Self-awareness is how an individual consciously knows and understands his own character, feelings, motives, and desires. It is the awareness of one's own personality and individuality.

γνῶθισεαυτόν

The above inscription is an invitation carved in the forecourt of the Temple of Apollo at Delphi of ancient Greece. It translates broadly as, 'Know thy self'.

This aphorism has been attributed to the famous Greek philosopher Socrates who taught that 'an unexamined life is not worth living'.

To put it simply, self-awareness is the consciousness of one's self and one's surroundings.

The authors of *How to Become a Better Leader* published in the MIT Sloan Management Review state that self-awareness is *the* most important capability that leaders must develop. Effective leaders know what their natural inclinations are and leverage this knowledge to boost those inclinations or offset them.

Self-awareness operates at three levels: *thinking, voicing* and *acting.*

Thinking involves contemplating about oneself and the surroundings. It is not as easy as one thinks. That is because more than 45% of our daily actions are habitual. What does this mean for leadership? Is it possible for leaders to develop self-awareness skills while leading a team? What it means for effective leadership is this: a self-unaware leader is like a bull in a china shop. He or she goes about the business of leading without consciousness of the self, the team members and the environment in which everybody operates. Resultant leadership will be of poor quality.

Exercise (Without thinking answer the following):

How are your feet placed when you stand? Straight, at 5 past 11 or 10 past 10?

Why is your star sales performer not performing up to the mark for the last two months?

What was the real reason for the heated discussion with your boss in the last meeting?

Chances are that the answers to these questions may not be easily recollected or known. It is so because we are not consciously aware of ourselves or the surroundings. We do not find time to observe and reflect, to pause and think.

Self-awareness is a rare gift that very few species in the animal kingdom possess. Humans are one of the lucky few, besides orangutans, dolphins, orca whales, elephants and magpies. Since it is a rare gift it is highly valuable. Collectivistic human societies have generally a lower self-awareness level among its people because the focus of social existence is not on the individual here, but on the group. India is a collectivistic society. Of late it is becoming increasingly individualistic and materialistic. Hence, self-awareness is weak leading to multiple problems, especially in leadership positions. At the thinking stage self-awareness may be cultivated by reading, actively observing, asking 'why', labelling thoughts and emotions, conscious breathing, and attention to body language.

Voicing self-awareness involves creating an ecosystem of journaling, writing down thoughts and reflections, creating an action plan, and speaking with a self-aware person.

Exercise

- When was the last time you maintained a diary/journal?

Never _______

Less than five years ago_______

More than five years ago _______

Am presently maintaining one _______

- If you did maintain or are maintaining a diary presently, how did/do you benefit from it?

____

____

____

____

____

____

____

____

Who is the self-aware person you seek advice from?

I don't need anyone to help me be self-aware _____

I don't have anyone but would like to have someone_____

I had someone but then we lost touch _____

I presently have someone as my self-awareness mentor _____

Set aside time every day to jot down the highlights, learnings, and lessons experienced that day. Self-awareness suggests that this noting down must be goal-oriented. Hence, your journey of discovery should be able to tell you whether you are moving closer or farther away from your goals as an outcome of improved self-awareness. For instance, if you become aware that your short temper is not only destroying team morale but also affecting employee churn it would be advisable to take corrective action toward the goals of improving team spirit and reducing employee turnover.

In life, one experiences different situations and challenges. The less self-aware person will react and will not be in control of his emotions. He or she is likely to be extremely depressed with failure or disproportionately excited by success. Loss of equilibrium is an outcome of poor self-awareness. A highly self-aware person experiences calmness even in the face of upsetting situations or people and exhibits equanimity in victory. Such a person first becomes aware of his/her emotions internally, then accepts it, and then tries to handle those emotions calmly.

A self-aware person is one who may not be in control of the external challenging situations but manages it in a manner that creates less disturbance internally. Self-awareness is about knowing one's strengths and weaknesses, one's bright and dark spots, one's clear and blind spots.

So being self-aware is not only being in charge of a given situation but also being unaffected emotionally and behaviourally by stressful external situations. This mindset helps in 'acting' instead of 'reacting' to difficult situations. The difference between the two is that the former is planned, thought-through and goal-oriented. The latter is impulsive, immature and ego-centered.

> "Between stimulus and response, there is a space. In that space is our power to choose our response. In our response lies our growth and our freedom," stated Viktor Emil Frankl, an Austrian neurologist and psychiatrist as well as a Holocaust survivor. Such is the importance of self-awareness.

Successful leaders know where their natural inclinations lie and use this knowledge to boost those inclinations or compensate for them.

A study by Korn/Ferry International found that self-awareness level of leaders affects the bottom line of their companies. Interestingly, women executives exhibited deeper self-awareness than male executives. With most board rooms across the world packed with males, it is quite possible that corporate leadership, financial results and governance could have been better than what they have been generally if women had been more widely represented.

The quality of one's life will often be determined by the level of one's self-awareness.

Though it is so important, self-awareness is very often taken for granted. We assume that we know ourselves quite well and we know who we are, and therefore, this is definitely not a skill that needs to be worked upon on priority to develop ourselves into exceptional leaders.

It is unfortunate that our education system has laid more emphasis on rote-learning, marks and grades while largely ignoring the commitment to help students become more self-aware.

This trend continues at the corporate level. Most corporates focus on training employees with job skills in order to deliver better results and scale up productivity. Of late, however, corporates are attempting to impart soft skills to their managers to help them interact better with customers and other team members.

Programs to increase self-awareness could go a long way in making the workplace more enjoyable and productive.

Let us see if you know who you really are by answering some basic questions.

- Have you ever tried to understand yourself?

____

- Why do you behave the way you do?

  ____

  ____

- When was the last time you actively *sought* feedback on yourself?

  ____

- When was the last time you laughed at yourself?

  ____

- Do you micromanage your team?

  ____

- Do you know how the team members feel about your micromanaging?

  ____

- Do you become defensive when you get feedback from the team/superior or peers? ______

- Are you a good listener?

  ____

- If yes, then what per cent of the time do you listen vs talk with your team members? ________________

- Did you say something to your team/peers which changed the way they behave towards you?

  ____

- Are you in control of your verbal and non-verbal communication especially in difficult situations?

  ____

- Is it always the team's fault when things go wrong? If not, then when was the last time you took the blame on yourself when some major mishap happened?

  ____

  ____

  ____

  ____

- Have you ever analysed your personality traits? ____

- Do you know when to use which trait? _______________

- What is your values compass?

  ____

  ____

- How many times in the past year have you stuck to the right "thing"? _______________________

If you have answered the questions above honestly, you may realize that it is not very easy to claim that we know ourselves well.

As leaders, your actions, words and gestures are being closely watched and they influence your team members in more ways than you can imagine. Hence, a leader who carries himself with full awareness on what impact he/she wants to make *with* the team will make a better leader.

For this purpose, one needs to be self-aware of not only one's strengths and weaknesses, i.e. not only what makes him/her effective or ineffective, but also how one reacts to different situations.

Self-awareness is the ability to recognize our own and others' emotions and to use this awareness to manage our own behaviours so that we may get the desired behaviour from our team members.

Hence, self-awareness also helps leaders control or moderate their emotions which effectively helps them to connect to their team members better.

As is evident by now, self-awareness is extremely empowering as it customizes your thought processes/emotions and aligns your behaviour in a way which makes the team members more receptive to accept your leadership.

> "Yes, love yourself. But also, analyse and be critical of how you think, act, and behave. Self-love without self-awareness is useless. Be accountable to yourself first."
>
> Anonymous

In a study of 17,000 individuals worldwide, a Hay Group Research found that 19 per cent of women executives interviewed exhibited self-awareness as compared to 4 per cent of their male counterparts.

> Psychiatrist Prudy Gourguechon presents the question of what happens without self-awareness. Among her answers:
>
> "You would be ignorant of your blind spots."
>
> "You would not know when and how your emotions are distorting your thinking."
>
> "You wouldn't know what you know and what you don't know, so you wouldn't be able to count on yourself to seek necessary additional information."
>
> "You would not be able to judge the effectiveness of your communications."

"You would not develop as a leader because you wouldn't know where you need to go."

Here are some methods to determine your self-awareness level:

Method 1: Employ 360° feedback in order to compare how you think about yourself at work and how others think of you at work.

Method 2: If your organization does not follow the 360° method, choose a range of people in your organization on your own (some of the respondents should be people negatively oriented toward you) and administer a suitable questionnaire. Compare this with your self-filled questionnaire.

Method 3: Benchmark yourself to a known successful leader within or outside your organization. Map self-awareness parameters and compare with chosen benchmarks.

Method 4: Seek professional evaluation of one's self-awareness level, either face-to-face or online.

Method 5: Employ a personal coach. The expense can become an investment.

Method 6: Conduct self-analysis using the Johari window method.

(In the interest of objectivity, remove all extreme outliers. For instance, a comment such as "You are a rock star" or "You are the worst leader ever" should be ignored. Also, be cautious of feedback giving you a 5-on-5 on every question. Nobody's perfect.)

Method 6: In case you can't have any of the above, you can ask a few of your close friends to answer the following questions.

Friends about You	Score (5 max)	You about Yourself	Score (5 max)
What are my strengths?		What are my strengths?	
What are my weaknesses?		What are my weaknesses?	
My behaviours limiting my progress in my career?		My behaviours limiting my progress in my career?	
How would you describe me to someone in our personal circle?		How would I describe myself to someone in our personal circle?	
How would you describe me to someone in top management?		How would I describe myself to someone in top management?	
How would you describe me to my peer group?		How would I describe myself to my peer group?	
Total Score		Total Score	

Analyse both the results and it will be evident how much you know yourself and what the blind spots are. Blind spots are those elements of yourself that you had no idea existed.

The results can be mapped on two parameters—

a) Similarities
b) Differences

List the similarities:

1.

2.

3.

4.

The similarities are the behaviours that you desire to communicate which are in sync with how your peers/team members perceive you.

Make a list of positive behaviours:

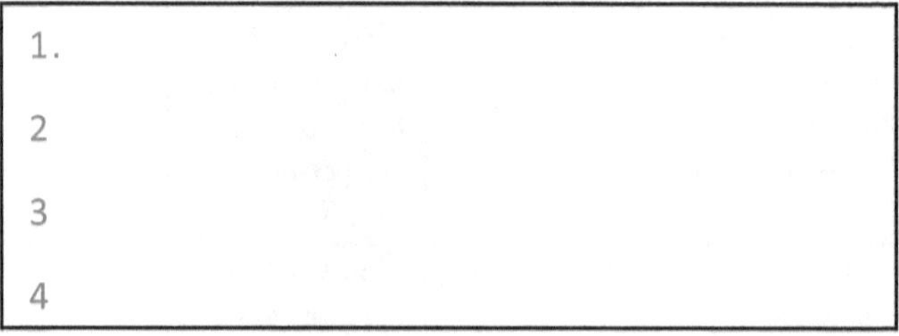

The above list constitutes your *sweet spot*, where your behaviours are making a positive impact in the minds of your team members and the team is benefiting from your presence.

The action point is to ensure that such behaviours are repeated more often so that your team members enjoy their work and go the extra mile to make the team more successful.

Make a list of negative behaviours (if any)

<table>
<tr><td>

1.

2

3

</td></tr>
</table>

Both you and your close friends agree on the above and you know that such behaviours are very detrimental to the team and to your own career and image. Such behaviours are to be aggressively controlled or eliminated totally.

It is going to be tough, and it must be done very purposefully.

> Tests to measure self-awareness must be capable enough of considering what goes on beneath the surface. Surface messages include vague statements such as, "I'm afraid", "They are unfair" or "I am trying to win". Deeper messages would be, "Afraid of what?", "Who is unfair" and "How are you trying?" These are specific in nature. Answers to specific questions help in improving self-awareness.
>
> What's in it for you?
>
> More self-awareness = More Choices

One method which has worked for us is "Flagging". We have often used flagging with our team by telling them that we have a specific bad behaviour characteristic (for example, tendency to get aggressive around month end) and that they should flag us whenever we get aggressive especially after the 20th of the month. We also assure them that they have our guarantee that they will never be penalised or punished for flagging us for that behaviour.

It took a lot of courage and swallowing of our pride, but it was one positive behaviour which made our team's and our work life enjoyable. You could give our version of flagging a twist by depositing a Rs. 100 note in the "Flagging Box" every time someone in your team flags you. Deposited penalties could be used to take your team out for a treat at the end of a quarter! When the penalties stop completely thanks to your becoming totally self-aware and in control of your aggression, then the *team* takes *you* out for a treat (hopefully)!

Such behaviour could build trust and camaraderie in the team and makes the team a formidable force.

Now the tricky part is when there are differences between what you think are your behaviours and what your respondents think is your behaviour. It is a dilemma. How should one go about dealing with such differences?

Let's start with the negative points about yourself. For example:

You: Believe you are a wonderful listener.

Respondents: Believe that you hardly ever listen.

In such cases, go by what your external feedback is. The simple reason is: perception matters a lot. What others think about you as a leader plays a prominent role in your long-term success. Because obviously, you cannot be a successful leader without willing and motivated followers.

Exercise:

Try to recall and analyse your behaviour in the last two or three meetings with your team and tick mark the appropriate responses below:

Behaviour to be Observed	How often do you do this?
How many times do you interrupt when someone else is talking?	Never | Rarely | Sometimes | Often
How many times have you paraphrased what the other person is saying?	Never | Rarely | Sometimes | Often
How often do you throw your seniority weight when there is a difference of opinion?	Never | Rarely | Sometimes | Often
Do you get emotional and defensive when someone else is disagreeing with you?	Never | Rarely | Sometimes | Often
What has been your body language during discussions/meetings/ conversations?	Bossy | Open | Relaxed | Supportive

And do the same as we did in the previous exercise to consciously be vigilant not to repeat those behaviours.

And the positive points mentioned about you, we should try to repeat them consciously.

Try this for 3 months and see the difference in the results. If done with full involvement and sincerity it will create a benchmark for all the other colleagues and leaders in the organization to emulate.

When faced with a difficult situation, the leader needs to pay attention to his or her emotions and be able to command control of his or her emotions and not the other way around.

Once in control of one's emotions, it will be easier to make an emotional connect with one's team members in a constructive and meaningful manner.

The Johari Window

Created by Joseph Luft and Harrington Ingham in 1955, the Johari Window technique is a useful tool to help people understand their relationship with themselves and others.

In the Johari Window exercise, subjects pick a number of adjectives from a list, choosing ones they feel describe their own personality. The subject's peers then get the same list, and each picks an equal number of adjectives that describe the subject. These adjectives are then inserted into a two-by-two grid of four cells as shown below.

The list of the 56 Johari adjectives:

able, accepting, adaptable, bold, brave, calm, caring, cheerful, clever, complex, confident, dependable, dignified, empathetic, energetic, extroverted, friendly, giving, happy, helpful, idealistic, independent, ingenious, intelligent, introverted, kind, knowledgeable, logical, loving, mature, modest, nervous, observant, organized, patient, powerful, proud, quiet, reflective, relaxed, religious, responsive, searching, self-assertive, self-conscious, sensible, sentimental, shy, silly, spontaneous, sympathetic, tense, trustworthy, warm, wise, and witty.

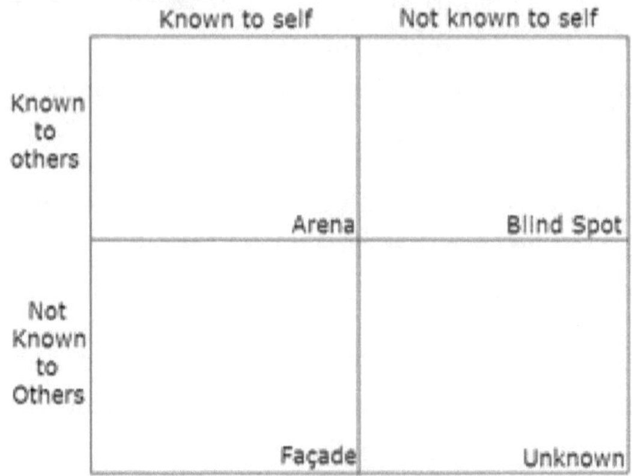

<u>Mechanics of the Exercise:</u>

Arena Quadrant

Adjectives that both the subject and peers select go in this *quadrant* of the grid. These are traits that subject and peers, both perceive. It is the Open Zone.

Blind Spot Quadrant

Adjectives not selected by subject, but only by subject's peers go here. These represent what others perceive but the subject does not. This is the Blind Spot.

The Façade Quadrant

Adjectives selected by the subject, but not by any of the subject's peers, go in this quadrant. These are qualities the peers are either unaware of, or that are untrue except for the subject's claim. This the Hidden Zone.

The Unknown Quadrant

The remaining adjectives which neither the subject nor the subject's peers selected go here. These represent the subject's behaviors or motives that no one participating recognizes—either because they do not apply or because of collective ignorance of these traits.

The technique is an engaging and enriching exercise in knowing yourself better and what others think of you. Take the test with a group of your colleagues.

Self-Awareness and Emotional Intelligence

Talking of self-awareness without reference to Emotional Intelligence (EI) would be only half the story told. Self-awareness is the first step toward EI.

EI, according to Daniel Goleman who popularised the term, is "the ability of individuals to recognize their own emotions and of others, to differentiate between different feelings and label them properly, employ emotional information to guide thinking and behaviour, adapt to the environment and achieve set goals."

The five components of EI important in business leadership roles are:

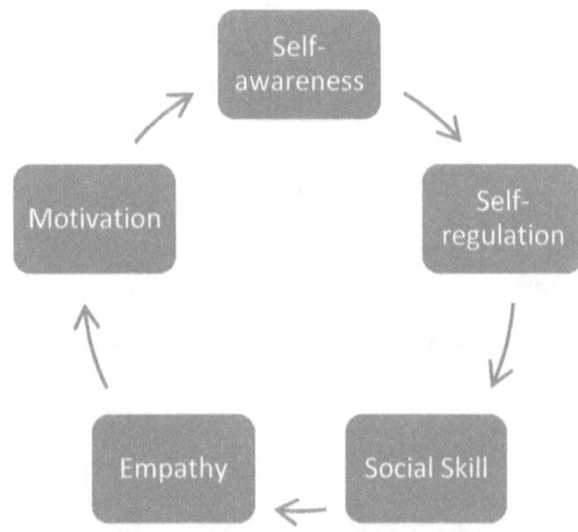

1. Self-awareness – the ability to know one's emotions, strengths, weaknesses, drives, values and goals and recognize their impact on others while using gut feelings to guide decisions.

2. Self-regulation – involves controlling or redirecting one's disruptive emotions and impulses and adapting to changing circumstances.

3. Social skill – managing relationships to move people in the desired direction.

4. Empathy – considering other people's feelings especially when making decisions.

5. Motivation – being driven to achieve for the sake of
   achievement.

Exercise:

On a scale of 1 to 5 (1 being the lowest) how would you
rate yourself on the 5 EI components?

SELF-AWARENESS	
SELF-REGULATION	
SOCIAL SKILL	
EMPATHY	
MOTIVATION	

What are the areas you would like to improve on?

____

____

What three steps would you like to take for each of the above
improvement areas?

____

____

____

____

____

____

____

____

____

____

____

____

Key learnings from this chapter for you:

1.

2.

3.

4.

X appears to be a friendly peer. However, he has the habit of shooting off emails to all and sundry in a rude tone if he does not like something or someone. If anyone retorts to his rude emails, he would quickly explain that he was misunderstood – "I was only thinking of the organization's interests". People in the organization see through his charades. Once in a while someone would retort in a similar vein. Such emails and retorts disrupt peace and are a result of poor self-awareness and low emotional intelligence on both sides. It is always advisable for leaders to be calm and self-aware when dealing with such situations. Tempting as it might be, one should not retort or take action without thinking. Self-awareness and emotional intelligence offers one the wisdom to step back and look at the big picture. The more one develops SA and EI, the better a leader he or she will become.

Self Awareness

It is how an individual consciously knows and understands his own *character, feelings, motives, and desires.*
It is the awareness of one's own *personality and individuality.*

Self-awareness operates at three levels:

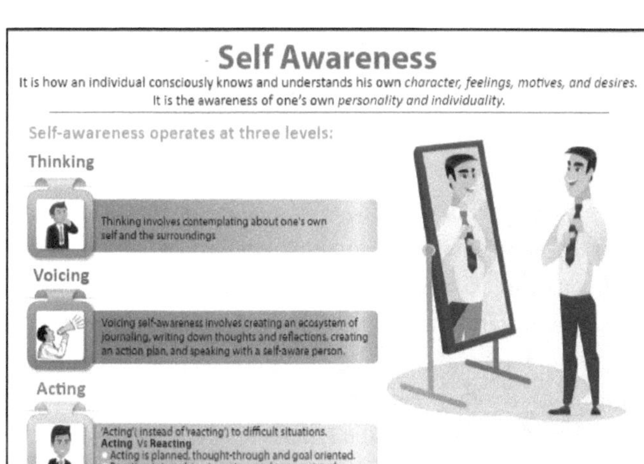

Higher Self-awareness = More Choices

LEADERSHIP ESSENTIAL # 3
SERVANT LEADERSHIP

"The servant-leader is a servant first... It begins with the natural feeling that one wants to serve, to serve first. Then conscious choice brings one to aspire to lead. That person is sharply different from one who is a leader first, perhaps because of the need to assuage an unusual power drive or to acquire material possessions...The leader-first and the servant-first are two extreme types."

—Robert K Greenleaf

Servant leadership is primarily about giving priority to team members' needs, helping them to grow as persons, and minimizing the negative impact of leadership on the less privileged in society.

The term 'Servant Leadership' may be a bit confusing.

How can a "leader" serve? Or how can a "servant" lead?

In other words, if managers start serving team members, who will manage?

Ken Blanchard, management guru and renowned author, emphasizes, "The problem is that folks don't understand leadership properly, leave alone servant leadership. They think that one can't lead and serve at the same time."

But of course, you can, if you understand that there are two aspects of servant leadership.

- The servant role : the "desire to serve" part
- The leadership role: the "facilitating to succeed" part

Hence, the servant leader begins with a service attitude and *then* makes it possible for team members to succeed through leadership. The first part is the service attitude and the second is the vision and implementation (the stuff of leadership).

According to Tom Peters, author of the path-breaking book on leadership and quality, *In Search of Excellence*, "Organizations should exist to serve. Period. Leaders should live to serve. Period."

The servant leader's primary objective is to serve the team members and take care of their needs.

This reminds us of a quote by the Nobel Laureate and poet, Rabindranath Tagore.

'I slept and dreamt that life was a joy. I awoke and saw that life was service. I acted and behold, service was joy'

Servant leaders take joy in their service. As a matter of principle, they put serving their team members before their own self.

Self-serving leaders are focused on serving themselves; they pursue privilege, power and prestige for themselves. Servant leaders are focused on serving others; they pursue privilege, power and prestige for team members.

Business stakeholders are now increasingly choosing servant leadership because they recognize that it is the right thing to do. There is a serious leadership crisis across businesses and this approach to a leader's role holds out hope that things can be improved.

How can you become a servant leader?

On the softer side, you can focus on two things to start with: *Your Words* and *Your Presence*.

<u>The Power of Words in Servant Leadership</u>

Words can make someone joyful or miserable; they can motivate or frustrate your team; they can honour or humiliate someone; with one word you can start a lifelong friendship or an eternal enemy.

The power of words or language is enormous, as it shapes the culture of the organization to start with.

A happy person at work is a happy person at home with his family, and a family is the very unit of our society in which businesses are embedded.

So, the words of a leader are indeed quite powerful as it has the potential to shape the organization's culture which can play a defining role in shaping the happiness of the homes and families of team members. Now that is an unusual thought. Since when did business leaders have the responsibility of ensuring happiness at home?! Well, for some time now that has been an important thought.

We remember genuine praise or a kind word for a lifetime and it has a chain reaction, as the recipient of a kind word often passes it around and it can cascade down to many others in the organization, creating a positive and happy atmosphere. This is not a clichéd, touchy-feely observation. It is something which works every time. Because in the end, human beings are more influenced by their heart than their mind, *ceteris paribus* (all other things remaining constant).

Words have energy and power; hence words have to be used with great care so that it becomes inspirational, and encourages the team to give their best to take the organization and team forward.

Hence, we need to be conscious and mindful of our words. As the famous Indian playwright Gulzar says, *"Lafzon ke bhi zayke hote hain; parosne se pahle chakh lena chaahiye."* (Words have many flavours; one must taste them before serving).

In the last chapter, we saw why self-awareness is a useful trait of a good leader.

Being self-aware ensures that we use words with caution so that it brings about peace and compassion.

Yes, sometimes we need to 'speak our minds'.

This means we need to be frank with an employee sometimes to give him or her honest feedback about their overall unsatisfactory progress.

In such cases, it is important to be mindful of what is to be said as emotions would be quite high on both sides.

Words need to be rehearsed so that there is no exaggeration of the issue, sticking completely to the facts; words are not to be used to put down or manipulate the person in any way. Instead, words need to be consistent and fair without letting personal biases come in the way of such conversations. Tough, yes, but with practice it becomes easy.

The suggestion to keep bias out of the communication is one of the key challenges for any leader or manager because it is very difficult to step back from a conflict situation and assess the problem purely on the basis of merit, away from personal ego. It takes prolonged practice. But is it worth it? You bet it is. Mastery of detaching yourself from a situation and addressing the situation objectively and then communicating the negative feedback to the recipient in a compassionate, empathetic manner is one of the best skills a servant leader can possess.

Exercise:

List three words that you use when as a leader you get upset with what you believe is a below acceptable performance of your team?

____

____

____

What has been the impact of these words on your team? Do they feel highly motivated? Or highly dejected? Does it serve your purpose of conveying your message? Does it create fear in them?

____

____

____

____

____

____

____

____

____

Do you think the right words have a key role to play in servant leadership? Why?

____

____

____

____

____

____

Other than words, we need to be conscious and ensure that we get the below three factors right when conversing in all situations, more so in such a situation.

Paying attention to the tone of your voice is extremely important, as words spoken in a kind and gentle manner conveys a different meaning than the same words spoken in a rough and derogatory tone of voice.

Your _body language_ is another aspect that has a profound impact on the effectiveness of your conversations.

A discussion on body language will be done in the chapter on 'Communication', but some basic points that need to be kept in mind are:

-   Use a neutral body posture
-   Look the other person in the eye in a non-threatening way to hold the conversation
-   Show agreement or disagreement from time to time (nod your head) to signal comprehension.

Actively listening and understanding the other person's point of view is not only fair but also shows respect to the other person who wants to convey his or her point.

Some basic pointers on how to be a good listener. (Details of listening skills will be dealt with in the chapter on 'Communication'.)

- Don't interrupt, be attentive, ask questions at the end to clarify any point and most importantly, please understand that listening is not the same as hearing.
- Hearing is a physical process of sound waves entering your ears. Listening is a focused and concentrated effort which is a mental process.

Active listening is not only paying attention to what is being said but to the tone of voice of how it is said, the words that are being used… it is about being conscious of the verbal and non-verbal cues that the speaker is sending out.

Almost all successful leaders and entrepreneurs including Richard Branson and Nelson Mandela credit their success to their listening skills.

The words we use, the tone of our voice, our body language, and our listening abilities are skills that need to be practiced. They go a long way in making a good and effective servant leader, hence, such skills need to be practiced over and over again.

Exercise:

Imagine your team has just had a big failure (like not meeting the monthly sales target). What words would you use to make the team members still feel enthused and motivated?

____

____

____

____

What words would you avoid while conversing with your team members?

____

____

____

____

____

A team member has exhibited poor team skills in a recent meeting. How would you communicate to him/her when 'you have to speak your mind'?

____

____

____

____

____

____

____

____

Do you think you need specific help on the use of proper words, tone of voice, body language and listening skills? Reach out to an expert.

What are your take-home points on the skills that need to be worked on?

____

____

____

____

____

____

____

The second way to achieve servant leadership is by leveraging your presence.

When do your people and team need you the most? Most often when they are in trouble or are stuck.

An important question that needs to be answered is, are you present when they need you the most?

Servant leadership is a reach-out program, i.e., when the team needs you, you reach out to them, instead of them having to reach in to you.

A reach-out program shows you care. It signals that you are aware of the issues that the team has to face in their day-to-day work and lives. Thus, the credibility and dependability of the leader is enhanced significantly.

On top of the above advantages, the reach-out program is time-saving and important issues can be addressed as soon as they occur or even *before* they occur.

Servant leaders make it a point to regularly drop in on employees and have informal professional or personal chats. They prefer face-to-face informal conversations to impersonal emails and semi-formal telephonic calls. In terms of servant leadership communication effectiveness, emails are the least effective, telephone calls are better and personal face-to-face discussions and personal handwritten notes are always the most effective.

The reach-in program (when the team has to reach in to the boss), has its share of bureaucratic and official delays in the name of hierarchy, protocol and processes.

When people have to reach in to the boss, there is a whole lot of explanations to be done. Hence, a majority of the issues are not brought to the notice of the boss, and is 'somehow' fixed by making it look as if everything is okay. Unfortunately, often they surface later and spin out of control.

Such mistakes can be very costly to the organization, which can be easily prevented if the boss practices servant leadership and reaches out to the team members more often by anticipating when they need help.

In contrast, if there is a self-serving leader, then he or she is more concerned about being served.

Servant leaders are more empowering than commanding.

A servant leader may not have all the answers but strives to create an atmosphere of empowerment and encouragement for the team to work together and find the answer.

Such answers propel the team forward as there is ownership of the action plan and people go out of their way to prove themselves right and hence be successful.

Servant leadership can create a bottom-up organizational culture instead of a top-down one. And even though it can be an organization- wide cultural thing, individual leaders can practice servant leadership within their departments, verticals, or teams.

> Lao Tzu wrote about servant leadership in the fifth-century BC: "The highest type of ruler is one of whose existence the people are barely aware. The Sage is self-effacing and scanty of words. When his task is accomplished and things have been completed, all the people say, 'We ourselves have achieved it!'"

Service is love made visible

Servant Leaders serve the people who serve the customers.

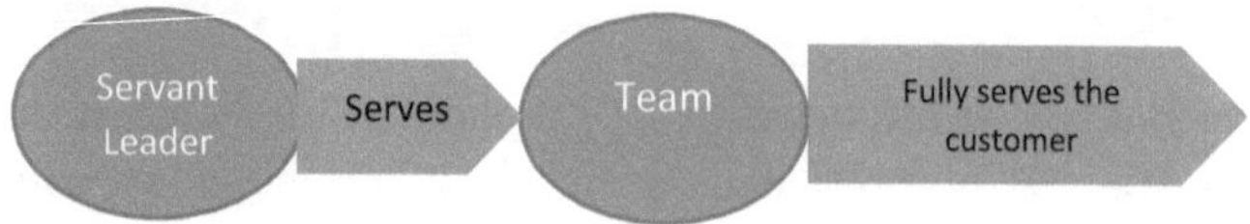

No wonder organizations which have servant leadership in their culture are so successful.

Imagine the other type of leaders, the ones who only wish to be served.

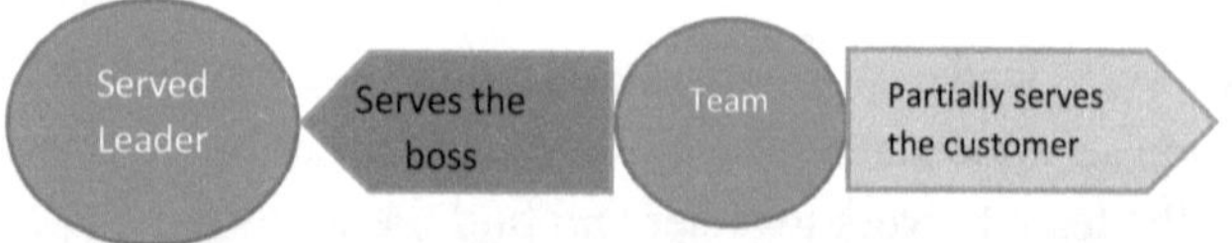

Here the team members' focus on customer service is compromised, leading to poor performance. They must serve the leader first and therefore their focus on serving the customer is compromised.

There are cultures where power is craved for. Once acquired, that power is used to make others serve the leader. All counter-points are demolished. All people who hold truth to power are suppressed and punished. History tells us that after some time, this approach becomes counterproductive.

In today's competitive environment it is very rare to have a sustainable advantage based on products.

The real competitive difference flows from the organization's people.

The people who are in direct contact with the customer (sales and after-sales service teams) are the ones that need to create the differentiation in the eyes of the customers.

It is but natural, that if the needs of the team are taken care of, if they are listened to and their requirements acted upon in a timely fashion, then it is highly probable that they will take definite steps to create value for their customers, take care of their needs, listen to their concerns and act on them. Isn't this what all customers want? Thus, in effect servant leaders can create and keep loyal customers for the organization.

SERVANT-LEADER BEHAVIOUR

The behaviour of a servant-leader is that of authenticity.

Behaviour is when the 'rubber meets the road' at the action point when a leader gains or loses credibility. Credibility is born out of "walking the talk".

The age-old saying, "trust has to be earned" is true. Even though a servant-leader has authority based on his position, trust is only generated through the servant and leader's behaviour.

Does the leader walk the talk or is it just a shallow show of concern and some pep talk?

Any doubtful behaviour by the leader is a breach of trust between the leader and the team members. Such behaviour doesn't go down well with the team members, and they become plagued by discontent. It becomes almost impossible to get them to believe in you in any future project.

In this way, you end up having a team which actually benefits the competition because the leader failed to instill trust and passion amongst the team members.

The results of a "service" attitude may not be quite predictable and definitely takes a long time to fructify, doesn't offer quarterly results or a measure on how it will help the company with the numbers. The tangibility of such a leadership style is questioned by traditionalists as it is mostly a "feeling" and doesn't lend itself to "quantitative assessment" easily.

In most organizations, going after the numbers game is the widely accepted approach. Numbers are easier to make sense of, is measurable, and therefore controllable and assessable. Going after the numbers is sometimes taken to be the mark of a strong leader, as a lot of energy is applied in achieving the numbers - which is the ultimate reason for which the leader is hired.

However, servant leadership is a different ball game. It is a more mature, long-term and empowering game for all stakeholders. But it needs patience and sincerity. So you have to assess whether you and your organization have patience and sincerity.

Being overtly focused on numbers makes a leader lose focus on the most important resource that he is being provided with to achieve the numbers, which is his or her team.

Servant leadership is about achieving numbers by leveraging a team with more empowerment, freedom, and risk-taking ability. Focusing only on numbers without taking care of the team can be disastrous.

WHO IS THE SPOTLIGHT ON?

We have been in presentations or programs with the chairmen or CEOs of organizations and it is a great opportunity to present yourself and be in the spotlight.

After all the leader has led the team to success and who else should be in the spotlight but him/her?

According to Robert Greenleaf, there are two extremes of leadership.

At one extreme is the "leader first", the leader who craves for the spotlight and uses it for the purpose of his or her personal advancement.

At the other extreme, there is the "serving leader", the "serve first" leader who turns the spotlight on the people and uses all his resources in making the team members exceed their own expectations by bringing out their best.

Below are some areas a servant leader is seen contributing to the team in terms of 'service'.

How to Become a Servant-Leader

According to Larry Spears, Former President, Robert Greenleaf Centre for Servant Leadership, these are the 10 most important characteristics of servant leaders—

Listening	Empathy-	Healing-	Awareness-	Persuasion-
Actively-listening to understand, not to reply	Feeling the other's pain/concern	Giving space to recover from failure/loss	Conscious of own strengths & weaknesses	Convincing the team of one's point
Conceptualization- Creating a vision for all to follow	**Foresight-** Knowledge of the future based on experience and wisdom	**Guidance-** Mentoring team members on the right track	**Commitment-** To Team's Growth Others before self	**Community Building-** Creating belongingness

Of the many approaches to attaining servant-leadership excellence, we recommend the following:

STEP 1	•Identify how you can support the team rather than imposing your expectations on them
STEP 2	•Empower your team to give feedback to you honestly on your actions as a leader
STEP 3	•Seek feedback instead of telling them what to do
STEP 4	•Avoid the desire to accumulate power in yourself. Instead try giving it away.
STEP 5	•Practise humility everyday with your team

THE STORY OF DAN PRICE AT GRAVITY PAYMENTS

Dan Price, Founder & CEO of Gravity Payments, a credit card processing company that serves independent businesses, once took a personal salary cut to implement a minimum $70,000 annual wage for his employees. Instead of his company being hit financially as he initially feared, profits increased. The icing on the cake, however, was when all the employees got together and bought Price a Tesla car. This is Servant-Leadership in action and its rewards.

Exercise:

What are some of the cultural elements of an organization that prevents the practice of servant leadership? (For eg., rigid hierarchy, authoritarian leadership, etc.)

____

____

____

____

In the last three months, how and when did you demonstrate servant leadership, if at all?

____

____

____

____

In the last three months, how and when did you *not* demonstrate servant leadership?

____

____

____

____

In hindsight, could you have handled the situation better as a servant-leader? How or why?

____

____

____

____

How well do you know your team members other than their work personas? Do you know their hobbies, their likings, their family members, etc?

Team Member 1

No. of Children & Names	Hobbies	Spouse's Name	Spouse's employment status	Last big milestone in their lives

Team Member 2

No. of Children & Names	Hobbies	Spouse's Name	Spouse's employment status	Last big milestone in their lives

In conclusion, we believe servant leadership creates long-lasting and deep personal relationships which go beyond professional boundaries and work-related issues.

The leader gets to know the team in depth, their strengths, how they behave in stressful conditions, their pain points and what energizes them and makes them perform.

Sometimes such bonding outlasts the professional association tenure as many successful servant-leaders will vouch.

Exercise:

Have you ever experienced a servant leader in your professional career so far? ___________

If yes, how successful was the team in his/her leadership tenure? Give some of your personal achievements while you were there in his/her team?

____

____

____

____

Can you describe what traits of a servant leader you want to imbibe or have imbibed from him or her in your leadership style?

____

____

____

____

Are you still in touch with him or her? Why?

____

____

____

____

> "Leadership is not about being in-charge. Leadership is about taking care of those in your charge".
>
> --Simon Sinek

Key learnings from this chapter for you:

1.

2.

3.

4.

Leadership in Times of Crisis

In the early 1970s, only six countries in the world had satellite launching capabilities. India was not one of them. Indian Space Research Organization (ISRO) was set up with a target of developing Satellite Launch Vehicles (SLVs) capable of sending up to 40kg payloads into a 400 km high orbit.

Prof Satish Dhawan, ISRO Chairperson, gave that responsibility to Dr APJ Abdul Kalam and designated him Mission Director. Dr. Kalam and his team of scientists worked for seven years to create the SLV from scratch.

While speaking on leadership, Dr. Kalam recalled an event from his ISRO days. "The year was 1979. As Mission Director for SLV3, I was ready to launch it. The countdown went to T minus 40 seconds and then the computer put it on hold. There was a glitch. Six experts behind me advised me to listen to the computer and postpone the launch till the error could be corrected." At that moment he had to make a decision. He made it. Dr. Kalam overruled the computer and SLV3 shot off into space.

Of the 4 stages of the rocket, the first stage went off well. It was in the second stage that it went off-plan and landed in the Bay of Bengal. 1979 SLV3 was a failure. Dr. Kalam recounts he was stunned and ashamed. He wondered how he would manage the repercussions of this colossal failure.

Just then a great man, a great leader, Dr. Dhawan approached the tired and deeply depressed Dr. Kalam and requested that he go with him to a press conference. At the press conference, to which Dr. Kalam went hesitatingly, Dr. Dhawan answered the press' queries and criticisms by stating, "Today we have failed. But I support my entire team so that next year they might succeed because I know I have a superb team." He took the entire blame on himself. The very next year, on July 18, 1980, when SLV was launched successfully, Dr. Dhawan requested Dr. Kalam to conduct the press conference, himself choosing to be in the background.

This is a story of how behind great organizations are great leaders. India was fortunate enough to have a great leader like Dr. Dhawan who headed ISRO and made India's space capabilities amongst the best in the world.

How to become a Servant Leader?

Servant leaders take joy in their service.
As a matter of principle, they put serving their team members before their own self.

Make your WORDS matter

- Words can make someone joyful or miserable; they can motivate or frustrate. they can honour or humiliate someone; with one word you can start a lifelong friendship or an eternal enemy.
- The power of words or language is enormous, as it shapes the culture of the organization to start with.
- Words can play a defining role in shaping the happiness of team members' homes and families.

Make your PRESENCE felt

- Are you present when they need you the most?
- It is a reach out program, i.e., when the team needs you, you reach out to them, instead they having to reach in to you.
- It shows you care.
  Helpful presence significantly enhances a leader's credibility and dependability.

LEADERSHIP ESSENTIAL # 4
VISION OF A LEADER.

"Vision" has been defined in many different ways but the one which we find most appropriate for working managers aspiring to be visionary leaders is this: "Vision is the ability to think about or plan the future with *imagination* and *wisdom*".

Vision is the very essence of a leader based on which organizations achieve great heights and make a difference in society.

Leaders conceive a powerful idea, envision it in detail, set the direction to achieve it and help team members to reach where they never believed they could reach.

Vision is about a dream in combination with action.

The vision of leadership permeates the workplace and is manifested in the actions, beliefs, values, and goals of an organization's leaders. This vision attracts and affects every employee who is engaged in living this set of actions, beliefs, values, and goals. They should want to share your vision.

> "Vision without action is delusion."
>
> - Thomas Alva Edison

In most organizations, many people can neither recall the vision statement of the company nor articulate what the vision of the leader is. Both are tragic situations.

Vision must be articulated clearly and forcefully at every possible occasion. In a large town hall meeting, the leader's vision must be elaborated in detail. During other opportunities, the vision can be put forth more briefly. And in yet other situations, the vision might be best explained by deeds rather than words. It also means that visionary leaders must have vision explanations set to different audience sizes to serve different purposes. For instance, if a merger is taking place, the leader's vision must be elaborate. On the other hand, if a new product launch has failed in the market place, it is hardly the time for launching into the leader's vision statement in a detailed manner. So choose your vision elaboration moment carefully.

In organizations, vision serves as a guide for the company's long-term strategic intent.

Vision is a *destination statement* supported by an *action framework*.

SpaceX designs, manufactures and launches advanced rockets and space crafts. The company was founded in 2002 to revolutionize space technology, with the ultimate goal of enabling people to live on other planets."

—SpaceX Website

Many worship Elon Musk of SpaceX (and Tesla, Boring Company and Hyperloop) as a visionary who has set the world on a radically new trajectory. Musk's leadership theme is "ideas". He is a visionary par excellence. Employees at SpaceX are in awe of Musk more than of SpaceX. An equal number of haters call him arrogant and delusional. But that is the lonely path that leaders with vision must embrace.

Managers are dime a dozen, leaders are available by the scores, but visionary leaders are a class apart. They are the gold standard of leadership. These are men and women of almost divine capabilities. Mahatma Gandhi, Jamshedji

Tata, Nelson Mandela, Steve Jobs, Martin Luther King and Swami Vivekananda were visionary leaders. However, it is not as if they were without any flaws and chinks. After all, they were human, but humans with the superhuman power to use their imagination and wisdom to craft a better future for humanity. The leadership vision goes beyond any written organizational mission or vision statement.

The ReCellular Vision

The story of a powerful vision is well explained by the story of ReCellular, Inc. ReCellular was a company that refurbished, repaired and resold wireless phones and other electronic devices and thus kept millions of kilos of these devices out of landfills, they also made hundreds of thousands of products available for re-use. And, they donated thousands of dollars to charitable causes from the profits they made from recycling.

For environmentally-committed people, this leadership vision was very appealing. The green mission and the opportunity to serve a cause bigger than themselves was a huge motivator for people to work for ReCellular. In addition, the opportunity to serve many charitable and environmental causes with the profit from sales of refurbished phones while working there appealed to another group of vision, mission-driven people.

(Source: Leadership Vision by Susan Heathfield)

A leadership vision is strong when the leader and the led both live the vision every day. That is very different from a few lines hanging impersonally from a wall.

What makes a Visionary Leader?

In an organization what should one do to become a visionary leader? Our prescription, based on an extensive literature survey, highlights the following:

- Lead with a dream of what the organization can become.
- Develop the ability to bring about unprecedented organization-wide cohesiveness.
- Fuse substance *and* style. Charisma is an essential ingredient of leadership.
- Display extraordinary confidence through track record and business acumen.
- Execute transformational change.
- Innovation and creativity should be the core strengths.
- Develop other leaders invested in the same vision.

Visionary leaders create a shared vision, which then gains momentum and the team moves forward towards its goal.

The quality of leadership is defined by the quality of the leader's vision.

Additive, multiplicative or disruptive change?

A leader must decide whether the vision plans for additive, multiplicative or disruptive changes? 'Additive' refers to visionary change brought about by a leader that affects only one's own department / business vertical. 'Multiplicative' refers to a visionary change that affects the whole organization. 'Disruptive' refers to a visionary change in the way the "business does business".

Does the vision take into account only the present challenges or does it also foresee the challenges of the future and has developed the inbuilt capacity to face those challenges?

Is it exclusive to one single vertical or affects the company at large?

Does the vision bring about a new way in which the organization looks at its business?

For example, a Walmart CEO a few years ago should have had the vision of an Amazon-dominated internet-based e-commerce retailing scenario challenging Walmart's domination in an omnichannel world.

The business world is playing in a very uncertain ecosystem now. Disruption is the given state of affairs. Additive vision is passe. Multiplicative vision is just about enough to stay in the same place without falling off the treadmill. It is a disruptive vision that will help a leader gain true respect.

Exercise

List one change you have brought about for your team / organization in the three categories:

Type of change	Description of Visionary Change Brought About by You
Additive	
Multiplicative	
Disruptive	

It is just fine if you do not have anything to list under disruptive vision change, yet. At least, this exercise should have put the thought in your mind as an essential ingredient for visionary leadership.

Vision is not permanent

Vision is not fixed. It can surely be long term but it can never be permanent. It may undergo alterations as per the demands of time and environment. This entails managing an organization over a period of time as the vision undergoes modification(s) due to intrinsic or extrinsic changes. Hence, it is important to keep all the communication channels open to convey the vision consistently and continuously to team members.

Communicating 'Vision'

Simply having a vision is not enough. The effectiveness of a leader is partly determined by how the vision is communicated to the team. This communication of vision is by its very nature different from normal day-to-day communication. Vision communication should excite, transport, stimulate, empower, sustain and visualize for the team members a future, better state of affairs of which they will be co-creators and co-beneficiaries. In today's times, it is also essential that leaders do not talk about the very distant future. Almost nobody, especially not the millennials, plans to be retiring from the company they are in at present.

The Effect of VUCA on Vision

This brings us to another valuable lesson: Visionary leaders should understand that any future planned goal of the company in an increasingly VUCA (Volatile, Uncertain, Complex and Ambiguous) world should not be more than 5-7 years at most. There is too much volatility, uncertainty, complexity and ambiguity in the business world. It will generate scepticism about any goal to be attained more than 5-7 years away. Employees today do not want to think *that* long into the future when a trade war or rising inflation or a burst technology bubble or political upheaval can wreck their jobs in a matter of days.

Strong Vision — A Call for Action

A strong vision when communicated properly, is a call for action for the team! It is a call for a marathon instead of a sprint. A visionary leader must be able to help develop the stamina required for a marathon as much as building excitement for the short sprints that are required to achieve smaller goals en route to the vision-goal. A visionary leader is a long-distance coach and a 100 metre dash coach both rolled into one. That requires extraordinary skills. Visionary leaders are extraordinary people.

Negotiation – A necessary skill

A visionary leader must also be a master at negotiating and overcoming resistance to change. Vision is more than a quarterly number that needs to be achieved. A vision is conceived, born and delivered to make a change from the status quo. This entails change. The cheese must be moved. A lot of influential people in the system end up becoming really upset. They draw their daggers to stab and sabotage your grand vision. The visionary leader must anticipate this overt and covert resistance. (S)he is not only like the military general who visualizes victory but also a leader who must make plans to overcome enemies from within. When established empires inside the organization are threatened, those satraps will come gunning. Often those internal battles will be fought in the boardroom. But they will also be fought on the factory floor and in office canteens. The visionary leader must have a team in place to bring about positive change in both places. He should have no illusion that the war will be fought only on one horse using a single sword. Once the internal victory is won, the fight for the market gets underway. Sometimes the reverse also happens. And of course, sometimes both happen in parallel. A visionary leader will, eventually, have battle scars.

Vision – Seeing the Endgame before the first pawn moves

Changing the status quo starts with dissatisfaction with the current situation. A visionary leader sets about channelizing this discontent into a dream or idea to steer the organization away from this harmful climate. These dreams or ideas are powerful enough to move people even before they take concrete shape. The visionary leader sees the endgame even when nothing tangible is in sight.

The Dual Creation of Vision

A visionary leader creates the vision in two stages: first, in the mind where the vision is born, nurtured and shaped; and second, in the execution phase where the concept is translated into action. The first birth is the more important event. The second birth will flow from the completeness of the first. If the first is complete and well-formed, the second one will most probably be done well.

Sometimes the team doesn't want to change from the status quo even if it is not totally satisfied with the current situation. Employees will be willing to change and make sacrifices only if they are convinced and believe in the vision. This is easier said than done as most visionary leaders will confess.

The dual creation of vision is an important idea that managers aspiring to be visionary leaders must bear in mind. It can prove a helpful guide.

Failure of Visionary Leadership

Visionary leadership is often unsuccessful because there are too many mistakes that such leaders end up committing.

One of the common mistakes that aspiring visionary leaders commit is to cause the burnout of team members with constant changes. Many of us have had leaders who change plans twice a day! Imagine the frustration and desperation in the team.

Another common mistake is treating all ideas equally. A simple mechanism is to grade the quality of an idea from 1— "an idea" to 5 — "an idea I am going to pursue no matter what". On that scale, 2 would be "a good idea"; 3 would be "an idea I am considering and detailing", and 4 would be "an idea that I will chase unless something more important comes up". This grading could help significantly alleviate the problem of communication and commitment.

Secondly, failure to offer appropriate progress rewards is a trigger for team members going off track and becoming demotivated. Without a high level of motivation, how can the long-term vision of a company be pursued? It must not be forgotten that followers do not have the same high level of investment in a visionary goal as a visionary leader. They are employees at a lower leadership level and need constant encouragement to move up. The leader cannot despair and become frustrated. A visionary leader must set short term goals which will add up to achieving the vision for the company.

The Vision Journey

The leader...

- Has a dream on how the future should be.

- Believes that it is possible.
- Formulates an action plan to achieve the vision.
- Communicates the vision or the dream to the team members passionately and consistently.
- Sets a direction and purpose for himself and the team members.
- Walks the talk and goes to work with a set action plan.
- Inspires and enthuses the team members to believe in themselves and work towards a goal which is bigger than themselves.
- Doesn't get discouraged when initially only a few people believe that the vision is achievable.
- Relentlessly pushes the action plan.
- Keeps on communicating the vision irrespective of the initial drag amongst the followers.

The above process will be quite challenging, to say the least.

To sum it up, according to Jack Welch, ex-Chairman of General Electric, "Good business leaders create a vision, articulate the vision, passionately own the vision, and relentlessly drive it to completion."

Leaders without a strong vision.

Now, imagine a leader without a strong vision.

How do you think team members will feel?

"There's nothing more demoralizing than a leader who can't clearly articulate why we're doing what we're doing."

—James Kouzes and Barry Posner, authors of *Five Practices of Exemplary Leadership*

Imagine a captain (Captain #1) of a cricket team telling his/her team members, 'Let's play our best and win this game'.

Now imagine another captain (Captain #2) telling his team:

"This is a very important game. If we win this game, we gain 4 points which will help our team secure a place in the semi-finals. This will give us a good chance to be in the finals, as we have to face teams which are relatively less skilled than us as per the draw. So the finals can be very much in our sight if we win this game. So let's give it our best shot."

Captain #2 has provided the team details of *individual ownership* and *milestones and how to work as a team* in a more visual way with a clear outcome – a place in the finals. The power of visualization helps team members with the required cues, the shiny hooks on which to hang their efforts for the next one or two years while the vision is pursued. The visionary leader must keep refreshing the visual imagery as sights might get blurred, or fatigue might set in over time.

Now another captain, Captain #3, provides even more details: Over and above what Captain #2 stated, Captain #3, says, "The opening pair needs to stay at the wickets for a minimum of 5 overs and score 70 runs. On hitting that target, Abhijit should get more aggressive and Aziz will give him more strike so that the partnership reaches 150 by the 15th over. Be careful of the spinner who is likely to bowl in the first 3 overs and the pace bowler who has taken 4 wickets in the last 2 games against us." Now, everybody knows what they have to do on the field. Everyone has accountable goals. There is cognizance of the competitor's strengths. Since everyone knows what everyone else has to do, there is complete transparency, and with that comes clear opportunities for collaborations between team members in pursuit of the vision.

Planning for eventualities:

Captain #3 goes on to build Plan B: "In case the opening pair gets out before the first over then Sunil will go in as 1st down instead of Vikas so that he can bring stability to the team. The revised target will be to score 50 runs from 8 overs and then go for the strike and achieve 120 runs by the 15th over."

OR

Imagine Captain #1 who says this:

"Our country where cricket is a religion hasn't won a World Cup in 15 years. We haven't stood on the podium and uncorked the champagne bottle in a long, long time. It's time we do that."

Which of the above three captains would you prefer and why?

____

____

____

____

____

____

____

____

____

____

Two aspects need to be done extremely well for a team leader to exhibit good vison to make a team win:

a) Setting and reviewing goals
b) Analysing competitors

Setting Goals

Each individual should be clear on his or her short-term goals so that they are milestones in achieving the bigger vision.

Short-term goals should be about a sense of achievement and reward for the team members so that they pursue the next goal with more enthusiasm with the sense that he or she is playing an important part in achieving a bigger goal.

This creates momentum for the entire team and momentum of this kind is a great problem solver.

Problems are bound to come up on the way to achieving one's goals, both internal and external.

Most experts agree that external problems no matter how big or complex can be solved when the internal problems are under control or internal challenges are met.

According to your experience, what are 'goals'?

____

____

____

____

____

____

____

What are the necessary elements of goal setting?

____

____

____

____

____

____

____

How to set goals is a very pertinent question and all leaders irrespective of their place in the hierarchy or span of control, should be a master in the area of goal setting.

S.M.A.R.T. Goal Setting

The acronym S. M. A. R. T. is an effective guideline to set goals and many successful leaders have used the SMART goal setting framework to get to where they and their team want to reach.

Let's learn more about the S. M. A. R. T. framework:

	Meaning	Description	Questions to be asked	Be Careful about
S	Specific	Clear goal statement; to the point; no ambiguity	What is to be accomplished? When to be achieved? Where and how is the goal to be achieved? What resources are required? Why is the goal important?	Fuzziness Indecisiveness Too many goals together

Now let's go through an example:

Stated Goal: I want to reduce my weight.

Is the above a specific goal?

Yes or No. ________

Why?

____

____

____

____

____

Let's re-work the goal (as you would have correctly pointed out, it is not a specific goal):

The "5 W 1 H" approach

"I (who) want to reduce 5 kgs (what) in two months (when) by going to the gym (where) so that I can be in shape (why) by doing cardio and weight training (how)."

It may not be always necessary to have all the W's and the H in the goal statement, but more the detailing, the more specific will the goal become for better and clearer understanding.

Let's take one more example.

"My (who) goal is to achieve Rs. 500,000 net sales (what) in the month of December (when)."

It has the *who*, the *what*, and the *when*.

But two W's and the H are missing.

The 'why' may be incorporated as:

"My goal is to achieve Rs. 500,000 net sales in the month of June to qualify for the special incentive earning (why)."

Still the 'where' is missing, which may not be too important to mention as it is implied that a sales executive will achieve his or her target in the assigned market.

But no harm in making the goal more specific to ensure that there is no ambiguity.

Now the 'H: How'

"My (Who) goal is to achieve Rs. 500,000 net sales (What) in the month of December from my designated area of Delhi (Where), to qualify for the special incentive (Why) by leveraging my strong relationships with five 'A' category customers so that I can increase my selling efficiency by 15% (How).

Compare and rate this goal with the first goal on a scale of 1–5, 1 being the lowest. _______

Give two specific goals that you would like to set for yourself in the next three months.

1.____

____

____

____

____

____

____

____

____

2.____

____

____

____

____

____

____

____

____

____

Check if it has all the 5 W's and 1H.

Now set three specific goals for your team for this quarter.

1.____

____

____

____

____

____

____

____

____

____

2.____

____

____

____

____

____

3.__________

Mark the W's and the H in each of the above goals.

Can you give an example of a goal set for the team prior to this assignment?

Would you like to make some changes to make it a specific goal?

____

____

____

____

____

____

____

M- Measurable

	Meaning	Description	Questions to be asked	Be careful about:
M	Measurable	Progressively trackable using well-understood metrics	What is to be measured? When and how often? Who measures? Why should it be measured with the given frequency? How is it to be measured?	Too much measurement; Ambiguity about what is to be measured

Goals must be tangible, where you can gauge progress by a specific number at pre-determined intervals.

Goal achievement needs to be tracked for progress and to monitor whether you are on the right track to achieve the goals in the stipulated time. Measurability is not an *end-game* measure but an *in-game* measure and you will know what per cent of the set goal you have reached at any given moment in time. This is essential to plan out resource allocation and mitigate manic pressure toward the end of the goal cycle.

Don't be ambiguous with statements like, 'will increase the sales by a great extent', 'will work out to get in shape', 'will reduce smoking' and so on.

Such goals are just bluffs, as you will agree that little or nothing gets done as there is no accountability for the end result.

Measurable goals look like this:

"Will increase sales by 20% this quarter over last quarter, with a focus on closing 80% sales in the first two months."

"Will reduce 5 Kgs in two months, 2 kgs in the first and 3 kgs in the second."

Write some *measurable* goals for yourself to improve on this quarter's performance.

1.____

____

____

____

____

____

____

2.____

____

____

____

____

____

____

3.____

____

____

____

____

Write some *measurable* goals for yourself to address some issues in your team.

1.____

____

____

____

____

____

____

____

____

2.____

____

____

____

____

____

____

____

____

3.____

____

____

____

____

____

____

____

Write three *measurable* goals for your team members that
you will give them to improve on their current performance.

1.____

____

____

____

____

____

____

____

2.____

____

____

____

____

____

____

____

3.____

____

____

____

____

____

____

____

____

Write three *measurable* goals for your team members to address some skill areas which need improvement.

1.____

____

____

____

____

2.____

____

____

____

____

____

____

3.____

____

____

____

____

____

____

A – Attainable

	Meaning	Description	Questions to be asked	Be careful about:
A	Attainable	Achievable; Realistic	Has my team done something similar before? Does the industry have similar goals? Does my team have the requisite skills to attain the goal? Does my team need new skills to achieve the goal? Who can lead in the team? What resources would be required? How much do we have to depend on other departments?	Being unrealistic Not matching skills required to attain goals Not accounting for dependency on other departments

Questions to be asked: Is the goal really attainable? Is it realistic?

Have you decided on a goal which in your heart you know is not possible, that it is over-ambitious?

'Reduce 20 Kgs in one month through my regular workouts.'

'Double the sales in this quarter over last quarter from the same geography with the same product range'

Most often, the above goals are unattainable.

When setting goals for self, one needs to be realistic and set goals with lots of stretches, while being realistic. That might seem like a contradiction. How can stretch reconcile with realism? Well, we all can figure out how much a rubber band will extend before snapping. The realistic point is just before the snap. You will see the snapping points if you know what to look for, like CVs of your team members out in the market, or fewer people coming to work highly motivated and enthusiastic, or a lot of gossiping going on instead of actual work. These are signals of snap points about to happen. Pre-empt such situations as a visionary leader.

When setting goals for the team or with the team, leaders need to make the goals mutually agreed upon. Mutually agreed upon goals are more likely to get accomplished.

However, though the goals may be mutually agreed upon, they should ultimately be a part of the whole objective of the company or the team's achievement, with an adequate element of stretches and challenges.

How do you usually give a "stretch" goal to your team members?

____

____

____

____

____

____

____

____

What has been the success rate when goals have been mutually agreed upon by the team members versus when goals have been communicated to the team members unilaterally by the leader?

Comment on the energy level and commitment of the team when there is an agreed goal.

R- Relevant

	Meaning	Description	Questions to be asked	Be careful about:
R	Relevant	Goal connected or appropriate to the overall organizational vision or mission	Is the goal aligned with a larger objective? Can the goal be completed within the time period of	Misalignment with corporate goals; Time stretch; Irrelevance to team members' perceptions of

			the larger goal? Is the goal in line with what team members consider important and urgent?	what is important and urgent

R- Relevant Goals

The goals should be relevant to the overall objective.

To use an analogy, if a patient has health issues and the doctor advises weight loss, and then if the patient sets up this goal: *'Will complete writing my new book in the next one month'*, it would have no relevance to the health objective which is important and urgent for the patient.

When *"increasing sales 20% month on month"* is an overall objective, then one needs to have a *sales* goal, instead of, *"I will work on my communication skills for the next one month."*

Although communication may have an impact on the overall sales in the long run, it is not a relevant objective in this case and team members will ignore it or be unable to focus on it given a larger pressing goal of increasing sales.

Relevance is about having a focus on the issue at hand and setting goals as per the need of the hour. But visionary leadership is about long term results. Hence, the lesser goals, or intermediate goals, must be aligned to the overall goal and help achieve the long term vision.

It becomes clear now that "relevant" goals are intermediate goals to address the issue at hand while on the way to the larger objective. They are like small rest stops up a hill to the summit. Suddenly digressing to see what's in the river valley off the main track not only makes the journey longer but distracts efforts and resources. In fact, many might find the river valley more interesting as one does not have to climb anymore up to the summit!

List two "irrelevant" goals that you or your team had to take recently which digressed from the main goal.

1.____

____

____

____

____

____

____

____

2.____

____

____

____

____

____

____

____

____

T- Time Bound

	Meaning	Description	Questions to be asked	Be careful about:
T	Time bound	Completing goals in a prescribed time frame; time is money; delays are costly	How much time is required to achieve the goal? Can we move faster if more resources are provided? Is the time frame unrealistic? What constraints can prevent achievement of goal within prescribed time limit?	Time extensions; Other departments making your team lag behind; Slow runners in your team dragging down the overall team speed

T- Time-bound.

A time-bound goal is more likely to be completed as it is known how much is to be done in a stipulated time frame.

Open-ended goals are not goals, but just wishful thinking with a low probability of success.

When a goal is set, there must be milestones set to the overall achievement of the final objective.

Consider a goal stated thus, *"I will reduce 10 kgs from my weight, by working out every day for one hour in the gym so that I get into great shape."*

This is an example of a well "intentioned" goal having no progressive milestones and no fixed time frame for the final achievement. Whether the goal is to be achieved in two months, six months or one year is any one's guess. Hence, the achievement will be stretched into the time available; in this case, time available is indefinite.

Naturally, it is highly unlikely that those 10 kgs excess weight will actually disappear.

Now re-write the same goal in a time-bound manner.

____

____

____

____

____

The new goal statement should look something like this:

"I will reduce 10 kgs of my weight, by working out every day for one hour in the gym and carefully watching my diet so that I get into great shape within 6 months, gradually increasing the weight loss as follows: 1 kg in the first month; 1.5 in the second; 1.5 in the 3rd; 1.5 in the 4th; 2 in the 5th and 2.5 in the last month'.

Doesn't it look so much more complete and do-able? One can measure the progress, on a monthly basis.

The owner of the above goal would be so much more committed and motivated to the progress, as the timelines for each little stop up the hill is specific, measurable, attainable, relevant and time-bound, i.e. S.M.A.R.T.

Corrective measures can be taken if the progress is not in line with the overall objective in a specified time frame. Visionary leadership is all about setting goals with time-bound markers. Some milestones will be tougher than others.

For instance, getting a 10% increase in market share in a highly competitive marketplace could be a visionary goal for a company which is always in the second place. A leader in such a company would have to appreciate that an initial couple of percentage points gain in market share would be the tougher milestones. Once the team gets early successes, motivation will get turbocharged. So in the first few months, the sub-goals should be smaller and with success will come momentum to charge on ahead towards the end of the cycle with the team achieving larger percentage jumps in market share. Like the weight dropper in our example above, the visionary leader should pace out the final goal intelligently and wisely keeping in mind his team's skills, hunger, and capability for a sustained fight.

Time-bound goals create focus, discipline and a commitment to the progress. Focus, discipline and commitment are critical elements in achieving any goal.

It is also very important to appreciate that while the team is at work, the visionary leader should lead from the front. He / she must walk the talk and lead by example. If there is a slippage in smaller goals, the leader must take action immediately. If there is a team member who is a weak link, he or she must be trained or exited. If the team needs resources or support from other teams in the company such as logistics or advertising, the leader should be able to liaison and pull in such support. If there is a major dealer / distributor / channel member that the team needs help with, the leader must go clear that roadblock. The leader must be with the team and be seen to be with the team.

Now that S.M.A.R.T goals are clearly understood, write three smart goals for yourself.

1.____

____

____

____

____
2._______________________________________

____

____

____
3._______________________________________

____

____

____

Write down one SMART objective for each of your team members, for which you need to get their acceptance in your next interaction with them.

Team member A

Team member B

Team member C

Team Member D

Now we come to the second important part in setting goals:

Competitor analysis

No company or organization can operate in a vacuum. Every company operates not only in an eco-system of current competition but also of future competition.

P.E.S.T.L.E (acronym for Political, Economic, Social, Technological, Legal and Environmental) factors are largely outside any individual firm's control and can present themselves as threats.

Hence, to have a competitor analysis, the leader needs to understand the macro factors (PESTLE) and undertake a thorough scan of it.

Michael Porter in his Five Forces Model has stated that the competitive environment within an industry depends on five forces-

1. Competition in the industry.
2. The threat of new potential entrants.
3. Bargaining power of suppliers.
4. Bargaining power of buyers.
5. The threat of substitute products.

Porter's *five forces* is a framework to analyze a company's competitive environment from a strategic point of view. A clear understanding of this is necessary for visionary leadership.

It considers the strengths, weaknesses, opportunities and threats of a given company (called the SWOT analysis). Strengths and weaknesses are internal and specific to the company – for example, culture, brand legacy, employee skills, manufacturing capabilities, technology level, etc. Opportunities and threats are external to the organization – competitors, market place, government regulations, currency fluctuations, political climate and so on.

A deep analysis of the above elements can help a company design a robust business strategy and formulate a vision for the company.

Can you analyse the 5 competitive forces that shape the industry you are in:

1. Competition in the industry.

- Who are your three main competitors in the industry?

C1

C2

C3

- What major marketing activities (marketing, R&D, channel development, etc) are they engaging in?

C1

C2

C3

- Name the top 3 customers for each of the top three competitors in your area of operations

C1

C2

C3

- What have been the competitors' major success stories in the last one year?

C1

C2

C3

- What new products have they launched in the last one year?

C1

C2

C3

2. *The threat of new potential entrants.*

- Name new companies that have entered the field in the last one year.
- Name their products.
- How successful have their products been?

3. *Bargaining power of suppliers.*

- Is there a scarcity of suppliers for supplies that are essential to the manufacturing of the products or services of your company?

4. *Bargaining power of buyers.*

- Do customers have an alternative to your products (benefit wise, price-wise)?
- Comment on the bargaining power of your customers.

5. *The threat of substitute products*

- Are you aware of some close substitute products that can harm your current business?
- If yes, then what are these close substitute products or services?

Agreed that complete knowledge of competition is quite difficult to acquire, but it is essential to formulate the vision and strategy of a company or team.

Now let's see how well you know your own company:

- What is the vision of your company?
- Do a SWOT Analysis of your company

STRENGTHS (Internal to the company)	OPPORTUNITIES (External to the company)
WEAKNESSES (Internal to the company)	THREATS (External to the company)

- Do a SWOT Analysis of your team:

STRENGTHS (Internal to the team)	OPPORTUNITIES (External to the team)
WEAKNESSES (Internal to the team)	THREATS (External to the team)

Do a SWOT analysis of your main competitor

STRENGTHS (Internal to the competitor)	OPPORTUNITIES (External to the competitor)
WEAKNESSES (Internal to the competitor)	THREATS (External to the competitor)

- Where do you think that your company's strengths can benefit from the weaknesses of your competitor?

Strength of my company	Weakness of my main competitor	Desired outcome

Management by Objectives (MBO)

In a modern corporation, setting objectives and pursuing goals according to them has been used as a technique for nearly six decades ever since MBO (Management by Objectives) was popularized by Peter Drucker. MBO is simply the amalgamation of three main activities which effective leaders would do well to adopt:

1. mutually agreed upon goals between employer / boss and employees
2. periodic review of the fulfilment of each objective in a constructive work environment and
3. distribution of rewards to team members according to their level of goal attainment

Leadership at world-beating companies such as Hewlett-Packard and 3M have credited the MBO approach for their continued success in the business world.

Annual Performance Reviews (APR) or Work Performance Review (WPR).

Professionally managed organizations must have Management by Objectives (MBO) based Annual Performance Appraisals, for every level of the hierarchy.

At the individual level, MBO is translated into Annual Performance Reviews (APRs) or Work Performance Reviews (WPR). APRs are management processes designed to measure the performance of individual team members against mutually agreed upon objectives based on quantitative and qualitative parameters. Leaders must be able to set these objectives objectively and in consultation with team members. Such appraisals are done at fixed intervals, most commonly quarterly and half-yearly intervals, culminating in the APRs. APRs are graded or scored and have multiple parameters to assess the progress of an individual employee.

The role of the effective leader in conducting APRs is to ensure that there are free-flowing and candid one-on-one discussions on all employees' progress with the reporting officers for the review period. Compliances, achievements and deviations are measured objectively against pre-set parameters. The APR discussions also help the leader and his or her team members to further work on a development plan as required so as to improve the overall deliverables in the coming assessment period.

Exercise

Keeping this entire segment on vision in mind, create a vision statement for your team.

The stated vision must be clear, inspirational, and packed with energy for immediate action.

Key learnings from this chapter for you:

1.

2.

3.

4.

Thoughts of two visionary leaders on true leadership:

"Our philosophy has been that most of the money we might ordinarily have spent on advertising should be invested in customer service so that our customers will do the marketing for us through word of mouth."

Tony Hsieh, CEO, Zappos.

"We foster a climate where the employee can deliver what the customer wants. You cannot deliver what the customer wants by controlling the employee. Employees who are controlled cannot respond caringly. You need superior knowledge and real leadership, not management."

Horst Schultze, Former President, Ritz Carlton Hotels

What makes a Visionary Leader?

Lead with a dream of what the organization can become.

Develop the ability to bring about unprecedented organization-wide cohesiveness.

Style & Substance
Fuse Substance and Style. Charisma is an essential ingredient of leadership.

Display extraordinary confidence through track record and business acumen.

Execute transformational change.

Innovation and creativity should be core strengths.

Develop other leaders invested in the same vision.

LEADERSHIP ESSENTIAL # 5
THE 4 C's

Four essential qualities of a successful leader are: Courage, Confidence, Conviction and Commitment (the 4 Cs).

Why are these 4Cs important?

Let us see the meaning of each of these terms as applicable to leadership qualities before we dive deeper.

Courage is:

"Strength in the face of pain or grief; the ability to do something that frightens one."

Confidence is:

"A feeling of self-assurance arising from an appreciation of one's own abilities or qualities."

Conviction is:

"The quality of showing that one holds a firm belief or opinion on something."

Commitment is:

"The state or quality of being dedicated to a cause or activity."

The 4Cs of Leadership

In our previous chapters, we discussed Integrity, Vision, and Servant Leadership which are essential qualities of a successful leader. These qualities cannot come to the fore fully if the leader lacks courage, confidence, conviction and commitment.

Courage helps successful leaders in displaying traits like integrity, well-articulated vision and the humility to exhibit servant leadership.

Courage and confidence are qualities which can be taught in the classroom or in a workshop just as much as it is developed by observing leaders within and outside an organization. It also comes from one's value system. A leader from an unshakeable values foundation is both courageous and confident.

This is the story of one of the authors. As a front-line sales manager at the beginning of a pharmaceutical sales career, he was leading a team of people some of whom were without work experience and with moderate academic track records. Many of them were the first-ever graduates in their families and came from very weak economic backgrounds. The job assigned to them was to go to well-established doctors of the city and explain the company's drugs and request them to prescribe the drugs for their patients.

In effect, they needed to talk about the "science of drugs" to well-qualified doctors who had lived and breathed science for more than 30 or 40 years of their lives! The feeling of low confidence was clearly observable in the team members. His job as the team manager was to instill confidence in them and make them communicate effectively and convincingly so that doctors prescribed their drugs to patients.

Now, that was quite a tall call. How did he achieve it?

The process was time-consuming and required a lot of patience.

His leadership style demonstrated how the pitch was to be presented, handhold them while they learnt the pitch and be there with them while they pitched, encourage them when things didn't go as planned, prepare them for various situations, teach them how to tackle objections, make them aware of the bumps that they would encounter, and praise them for every small success.

The process was quite strenuous but with persistence, the results gradually became visible. The leader's courage and confidence was gradually transferred to the team members.

Confidence killers

One common confidence-killer is the attempt by leaders to assign big tasks to beginners. Beginners need to be assigned work suitable to their skill level; otherwise, leaders would be setting them up for failure. It is intelligent to assign them easier tasks in the beginning so that initially the confidence is built and not shattered. This needs courage especially in sales-driven organizations where every person is expected to be hands-on-board irrespective of their readiness. Very few managers have the courage to assign work according to the skills of members.

Confidence is like a muscle

Confidence is like a muscle one builds slowly with regular exercise. It is better to start small and build the exercise regime over time so that the muscles become well developed. Lifting of heavyweights when bone structure and muscle mass are not well developed can have disastrous outcomes. Similarly, like the gym trainer, the leader must gauge the capacity of the individual to take on a task and customize the level of work out and build the regimen gradually.

Can a leader develop confidence? Is it decided at birth or early childhood? Does leadership come only after one becomes confident?

Important questions. Yes, leaders can develop confidence and it is not absolutely true that only confident persons can become leaders. There are many less confident people who have been given leadership positions. They have then gone on to become great leaders.

We believe that like any skill, confidence can be acquired and developed.

The basic tenet of confidence-building

Practice: "Practice makes perfect" is an old saying. We believe "proper" practice makes perfect. One cannot become Sachin Tendulkar — one of the world's most celebrated cricketers or Mary Kom — world boxing champion even in her mid-thirties and as a mother of three kids, simply by practising night and day with a cricket bat or a pair of boxing gloves. One must practice *properly*. The proper coach, the proper moves and the proper mental attitude are essential. That is where a good quality leader comes into play.

Persistence: The art of continuing towards your goal despite repeated failures. This is one of the most desirable qualities in a leader. Success does not come easily. A leader must march on ahead. However, constant monitoring of the situation must be taken up. But a leader must avoid controlling employees. Controlled employees lose their initiative. If there are major changes in the environment or the team, like when a star performer leaves the organization, then the leadership must accommodate and adjust to the change. If the market has moved on to something else, then it would be futile to continue to persist with the same plan. Wisdom and intelligence tempered with humility to accept that a change of plans is called for, are the hallmarks of a great leader.

Self-talk: Motivating your soul through positive mantras spoken to yourself is very essential. Practice self-talk in your mind. Pepping yourself up with positivity is a good formula to remain courageous and confident, committed and convinced about your vision and mission. It is an effective technique as leadership often gets lonely.

Self-affirmation: Considered the world's greatest boxer ever, Muhammad Ali was often boastful. Whenever he talked to the press or his opponent in the ring, "I Am the Greatest" was one of his popular claims. This was actually self-talk and self-affirmation. It was, of course, backed up by a string of knockouts delivered to his adversaries with unfailing regularity. His courage was also on display when he refused to be forcefully conscripted into the US Army for the American War in Vietnam in 1966 stating that the Vietnamese people were not his enemies. This was a very bold stand at that time, for which he was stripped of his World Champion title and banned from the boxing ring for nearly 4 years of his prime fighting time. Courage has its price. Are you ready?

"I am the captain of the ship and master of my fate," brave words spoken on behalf of your team and yourself. Blame no one else for your failures and offer credit generously to all those who helped you reach where you are today.

Write a letter to your own self – all that is good about yourself. Don't be shy. Don't be bombastic either. Just state it as it is. Be honest and sincere when you write. List your achievements, and read them to yourself at those times when no one else believes in you. First, a great leader must believe in himself / herself. Only then will others believe in him or her.

Reflection: In the highly pressurized life of a leader in the current corporate context, reflection is a lost art. Reflection helps you step back from the everyday situations of leading a team, achieving numbers and reaching your vision. Reflection is a vital step in the self-improvement process. Irrespective of the time in the night when you finally rest, every day one must spend a few allotted minutes for reflection. It will give you the desired perspective. And perspective is not to be taken lightly. It adds depth and width, relevance and context of one's leadership style for the team that is being led.

Giving and Receiving Feedback: As a leader of your team, have the courage to praise positive behaviour and the courage to call out negative behaviour. Do the praising with openness. Do the calling out (reprimanding) in the privacy of a one-to-one. Courage in leadership refers to the ability to take negative feedback in a positive manner. This requires strength of character and confidence. In fact, courage in leadership is about setting up feedback channels, as formal or informal as desired, with the assurance of anonymity and no bar on the frequency of feedback.

In business, confidence is all about self-assurance which comes from expertise or good results. Expertise comes from knowing the product, the company, the channel, the industry, the consumer, the economy, the competition, the brand's history, government rules and regulations, and so on. Results come from repeated and successful performances in terms of important company objectives, especially in tough market conditions. An individual aspiring to develop into an effective leader needs to focus on both expertise and results. One without the other or neither is a recipe for failure.

Practice Exercises:

1. Write a letter to yourself about all that is good about you. Highlight all achievements, all the obstacles that you have overcome. List the people who appreciated your work or efforts. Make it as clear and bold as you can.

2. How confident are you about facing life in general?

    ____
    ____
    ____

3. What qualities do you already possess which make you confident about facing life (list at least 3)?

    ____
    ____
    ____
    ____
    ____

Confidence: A Must Have Quality

Confidence is often listed as a 'nice to have' quality, instead of as a 'must have'.

Have you seen teams or companies with a high knowledge base, and sufficiently well-resourced with 'skilful' people but still producing average results? They are more common than what one would believe.

'Confidence' may have been the missing ingredient from the equation.

What is the use of all the knowledge and resources if they are not going to be put to use to discover and unearth the potential of team members?

Courage is essential for change in order to keep up with the demands of the market place and the demands of internal customers. Confidence is the belief in one's own and the team members' strengths.

Doing things according to 'past practice' in a company and expecting to overcome new challenges may not lead to success in leadership. As they say, "If you keep doing the same things, you will get the same results".

But change is a difficult thing to bring about as the human psyche resists anything that it is not comfortable with, and change has its share of discomfort as 'new beginnings are often disguised as painful endings' (Lao Tzu). What this essentially means is that before the sun, must come the rain. When the rain comes, believe that the sun will shine soon enough.

Being able to take a stand and promoting practices and work norms which have not been practiced before takes lots of courage and confidence on the part of the leader as there is no guarantee that the changes will bring definite results.

Acknowledging that changes are required, but at the same time knowing fully well that such changes are not a guarantee for the desired result, and still driving the change speaks a lot about a leader's courage and self-confidence.

***Performance with purpose.**

Indra Nooyi took over as CEO of Pepsico in 2006.

She envisaged the shift in consumer behaviour and governmental pressure to limit the sale of sugar-based beverages and foods and the move to healthier options. Many governments including India in 2018 introduced the sugar tax for foods and beverages having a high level of sugar. In October 2019, Singapore banned advertisements of high sugar products.

Nooyi being a visionary business leader, introduced a new strategy at Pepsico: 'Performance with Purpose', and introduced healthy food and beverages.

Industry analysts told her, 'Don't be Mother Teresa. Your job is to sell soda and chips.'

She followed her conviction with courage and transformed the company.

Pepsico's arch rival, Coca-cola, stuck to their sugar-based soft drinks.

End result: Pepsi's stocks grew by 70% since 2011, and Coca-Cola's grew by just 15%.

A great example of courage and conviction in a leader.

Nooyi declared, "We are committed to delivering top-tier performance while being responsive to the needs of the more than 200 countries and territories we serve around the world. That commitment — what we call *Performance with Purpose* — is about expanding our portfolio of more nutritious products with the aim of shrinking our environmental footprint as a responsible corporate citizen and working to lift up people and families, from widening the circle of opportunity to providing relief in times of need."

Source: Pepsico website.

Conviction – When leaders stick their necks out

Courageous leaders with conviction have a huge impact on the team. In tough times, when the industry is sluggish and there are layoffs, most managers would like to keep their heads down, keep their mouths shut and make the 'least noise' so that no unwanted attention falls on them. They prefer to remain quiet till the storm passes, often not even fighting for their team members who get laid off. Without a doubt, these are the times when leadership with conviction needs to be exhibited. However, it is easier said than done; in fact, for some leaders, it can be quite frightening to stick their necks out for their team members.

When embarking on a new project, challenging the status quo, knowing that it's the right thing to do even though there is no guarantee that the project will be a success, is indeed unsettling, especially in difficult times. There is so much at stake. The fear of failing, the fear of losing one's job, one's career getting affected, and so on are some of the challenges that demand conviction in leaders.

Playing it safe is the preferred thing. Survival is the name of the game. Heroes who stick their necks out are remembered for a few days and the tide moves on. Is it even worth it? It might be useful to remember that "playing it safe" is a short term remedy in most cases. There are leaders out there who are bringing about disruptive changes, so as to challenge the status quo, aimed at the long term.

Let's see an example of courage which changed the trajectory of entertainment business models.

The cable is a rigid medium, where one had to watch whatever was broadcast, with no way to skip advertisements, no fast forward options to eliminate what one did not want to watch, no replay options of what one wanted to watch again, and it was restricted to largely one device – the TV.

Netflix, Inc., an American media services provider, headquartered in Los Gatos, California, founded in 1997 by Reed Hastings and Marc Randolph in Scotts Valley, California disrupted the cozy world of cable TV operators.

Cable companies were continuing with their normal business and were oblivious of the changes in consumer behavior, choices in entertainment consumption and the upcoming technological advancement. They were comfortable with a steady flow of business. Then came the disruption. Netflix bulldozed them out of business.

The challenger took into account the prevalent dissatisfaction of cable TV customers. They took advantage of the cable TV ecosystem which was anything but dynamic and customer-centric.

Netflix addressed the big customer pain points. It utilized internet streaming technology, eliminated geographical boundaries, it could be accessible from anywhere in the world, and it could be watched on any device. In addition, it adopted an innovative subscription based business model which satisfied the customer question, "Why should we spend our money upfront in buying a product when we can simply subscribe to one that can be switched on or off as per our convenience and need?" So, Netflix's business model was designed to be viable even if the economy slowed down. The subscription model was futuristic and it is predicted that it would undeniably capture a gross market of $100 billion by the end of 2020.

Result:

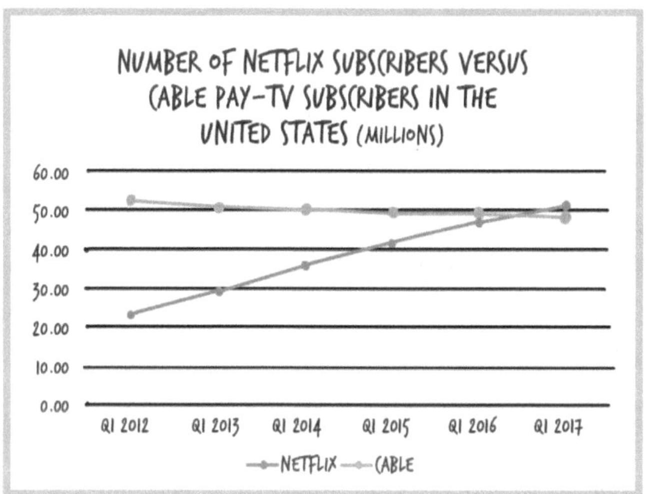

Sources: Netflix, Leichtman Research Group (Richer, 2017)

The above story is of a company whose leaders showed deep conviction and commitment, courage and confidence in their disruptive model of business by keeping their eyes open for customer pain points and acting upon them.

Team members will follow a leader not only because of his or her vision or his knowledge or qualifications but mainly because of the courage and commitment that the leader exhibits in real situations.

It is difficult to be an effective leader without commitment and courage. They are the attributes of a leader which inspire team members to believe in the vision.

The mission and vision are lived by the leader when the team members see him or her in action going that extra mile consistently and exhibiting commitment unflinchingly, especially when it is uncomfortable. For instance, if the market signals that a once-successful product category (such as tobacco) or consultancy practice (like energy strategy) is losing relevance with customers and the team associated with it is in jeopardy, then the leadership must have the commitment to defend, protect, reskill, realign and re-motivate the team. Commitment is visible when the leader stands by the team. It comes before success and often before all things get perfect. The leader's commitment opens the doors to achievement.

Communication consistency

Communicating the mission and vision clearly and consistently is important, but for the team to believe you and to be led by you, one must exhibit consistency in his or her commitment. A leader cannot follow one path one day and another on another day unless he has taken the whole team into confidence.

Consistency is also exhibited by how the leader deals with different team members. Often there are one or two members in a team who have their own ulterior agendas. A leader must stand up and take action against such people. Otherwise, consistency is not the quality the team members see in the leader and that could lead to negative consequences.

A committed leader walks the talk

A leader's commitment is measured by his or her actions. Actions must replace words on almost every occasion. Walking the talk inspires as well as gives proof of the leader's courage.

If a leader expects commitment from his or her team members, then he or she needs to exemplify commitment day in and day out.

A team leader who consistently tries to develop his or her own skills is likely to inspire the team members to develop their skills.

A good example of this would be the Indian National Cricket team captain, Virat Kohli. His commitment to keeping himself fit and agile is a standard that others are not only inspired by but must also achieve as a minimum requirement to be included in 'his' team.

Exercise

1. What are the areas you feel proud of yourself that you have walked the talk in the last 2-3 months?

    ____

    ____

    ____

    ____

    ____

2. What are the areas you would like to walk the talk in the next 2-3 months?

    ____

    ____

    ____

    ____

    ____

3. How do you think your team members will perceive you
    once you have accomplished the above?

____

____

____

____

____

Commitment and Accountability

Accountability is what makes a person stand out and be a
leader.

The leader is willing to make a difference by setting high
standards, committing to the set standard and then working
relentlessly at making it a reality.

He or she takes the blame if things go wrong and pass on
the credit to the team members in times of success, thereby
motivating them to commit to the cause for future success.

In the process, the entire team holds themselves accountable
as their leader takes ownership and accountability for
achievement.

Exercise

1. What are the areas you hold yourself accountable for?

____

____

____

____

2. What are the areas you think that you are not accountable for, but your superior thinks otherwise?

____

____

____

____

3. What are the areas you hold your team members accountable for?

____

____

____

____

4. Are there similar feelings amongst your team members, as in question 2?

____

____

____

____

5. How do you think that this conflict / disagreement can be resolved?

____

____

____

____

Committed leaders find solutions not excuses

Excuses are addictions. Harmless at first, they change our willpower swiftly and we become enslaved.

It is quite often seen that the underperformance is covered up with excuses by a leader.

What credibility or respect do such leaders have in the eyes of their team members?

A very common cover up experience is with sales numbers.

It is easy for the leader to cover up by saying that the economy is down, or that competitors' sales graphs are also dipping; it is so soothing and comforting to know that we are all sailing in the same boat and we need not feel guilty as it is the 'environment' which has resulted in the low sales volume.

In a matter of life and death, such as your need to support your family in a layoff situation, what does one do? Many solutions will present itself when it is a matter of life and death. Maybe you would work an extra shift, or partner with some relatives and friends and work with them and so on. Just because you got laid off does not mean that you can resort to finding excuses.

Similarly, when sales are down, the committed leader will find solutions to overcome the setback. He or she should ask questions such as:

- Can we make some extra calls to our existing customer base asking them to support the company in our tough times?
- Can we run a campaign for our highest selling product and try different sales channels?
- Can we explore a different market so that it can begin giving sales from next quarter onwards?
- Can we identify 5 top competitor's customers and work on an engagement plan with them?

The list of questions / opportunities goes on. It will soon be clear that the solutions are not really very tough to figure out. They are ordinary work plans with some creativity and extraordinary will. Such solutions when rolled out to the team by a committed leader energizes the team members and the entire unit goes out and hunts for more sales.

Solutions with an action plan have the power of a hunter, and a skillful and committed hunter rarely goes hungry.

You will agree that every day such opportunities present themselves abundantly. Effective leaders by their nature and training, commit to solving the issue at hand. Such situations clearly separate the problem solvers from the excuse givers.

Hence, to differentiate yourself from the average leader, commit yourself to solving problems, and you will have a dedicated team to work with, who will also commit themselves and raise the performance bar.

Exercise

1. List the solutions that you have given to the team and their corresponding results in the last 2-3 months.

Issues	Proposed Solutions with an action plan	Implementation Levels	Results Achieved
Eg. Proposal for increased funding not being approved	Determine roadblock; strategize to overcome it; failing this look for an alternative funding source	Team and immediate superior level; Seek help from other teams	Roadblock identified. Finance dept helped in reallocating budgets from another less important project

2. What are the issues that your team is facing that you wish to tackle over the next 2-3 months?

Issues	Proposed Solutions with an action plan	Implementation Plan	Results Expected

Key learnings from this chapter for you:

1.

2.

3.

4

Stories of courage and dedication.

(Reprinted from Space India, Oct-Dec 2003)

The President of India, Dr A P J Abdul Kalam visited the Satish Dhawan Space Centre (SDSC) SHAR at Sriharikota on October 10, 2003.

It may be recalled that Dr. Abdul Kalam was the Project Director of India's first Satellite Launch Vehicle, SLV-3, which was successfully launched from Sriharikota in 1980.

Since then, ISRO has come a long way in establishing the capability to launch remote sensing satellites into polar orbits using PSLV and communication satellites (upto 2 ton class) into Geosynchronous Transfer Orbit using GSLV, thus making the Indian Space Programme self-reliant.

After his visit to the launch facilities, the President addressed the personnel of SDSC at Dr. Ambedkar Open Air Theatre.

He cited several instances of individuals' commitment and dedication to the task of the nation's space programme at various levels, which have made India self-reliant in this technology. While appreciating the achievements of ISRO, Dr. Kalam said that ISRO has an important role to play in making India a developed nation by 2020, especially in the areas of resources survey, communications and meteorological services.

Excerpts from the speech of the former President of India, Dr APJ Abdul Kalam.

"At every stage, SLV-3 team was blessed with some extraordinarily courageous people.

Once Mr. Shivakaminathan was bringing the C-band transponder from Trivandrum to SHAR for integration with the SLV-3.

The SLV-3 launch schedule was dependent on the arrival and integration of this equipment.

On landing at the Madras (now Chennai) airport, the aircraft in which Mr. Shivakaminathan was traveling, skidded and overshot the runway. Dense smoke engulfed the aircraft. Everyone jumped out of the aircraft through emergency exits and desperately fought to save himself or herself — all except Mr. Shivakaminathan who stayed in the aircraft till he removed the transponder from his baggage. He was among the last few persons to emerge from the smoke and he was holding the transponder close to his chest. This is the level of dedication and the attachment to the project because people owned this project."

Dr. Kalam went on to say, "Another incident I remember is the one that happened during the third launch of SLV-3. The countdown sequence was proceeding smoothly. There were two operations to be carried out on the launcher — one, for release of the spacecraft's umbilical cord and the other, to release the arms holding the vehicle. Both these were pneumatically operated systems remotely controlled from Block House.

The arms got released as expected. However, the spacecraft's umbilical cord release system failed to respond to the command. This automatically stopped the countdown. There was suspense on how to proceed. The launch managers huddled together to find a solution. Mr M R Kurup and I volunteered to reach the umbilical system through a ladder to manually release it.

Seeing the situation, one young tradesman of SHAR, Mr. Pappaiah, volunteered to climb onto the launcher and release the mechanism manually. After clearance by the launch managers, he accomplished the marvellous feat and the vehicle was launched that day.

I can never forget such committed individuals who have become the backbone of ISRO."

Four essential qualities of a successful leader are Courage, Confidence, Conviction and Commitment (The 4 Cs).

● **Courage is:**
"strength in the face of pain or grief; the ability to do something that frightens one".

● **Confidence is:**
"a feeling of self-assurance arising from an appreciation of one's own abilities or qualities".

Conviction is:
"the quality of showing that one holds a firm belief or opinion on something".

● **Commitment is:**
"the state or quality of being dedicated to a cause or activity".

LEADERSHIP ESSENTIAL # 6
COMMUNICATING FOR SUCCESS

Once upon a time, in a mid-sized agriculture produce marketing company, one team member, who was originally a passionate and committed part of the team, had become detached and was slacking off. Torn between letting her go and keeping her, a one-on-one meeting was set up by the leader of the organization. It was only then that it was found that she was feeling left out of decision making as nobody had contacted her for months assuming that she being a passionate and committed member would be fine. Her long term goals had also changed over the past one year while the leader and her managers were assuming that all the assignments given to her were helping her achieve her previously stated long term aspirations. The power of one-on-one communications should not be underestimated, especially with smart and sincere employees.

For leaders to be effective, simply being eloquent and aware of the mechanics of communications is not enough. Yes, it is a 2-way process and yet it is much more than that. Communications is a core skill of effective leaders. The power of the spoken and written word is immense and can never be overstated. It can move armies of demotivated and frustrated employees into conquest. It can energize a team into delivering more than their best. It has the capability of transforming organizations. Conversely, a leader with poor communication skills can cause demotivation and insecurity and a lack of clarity and focus among employees.

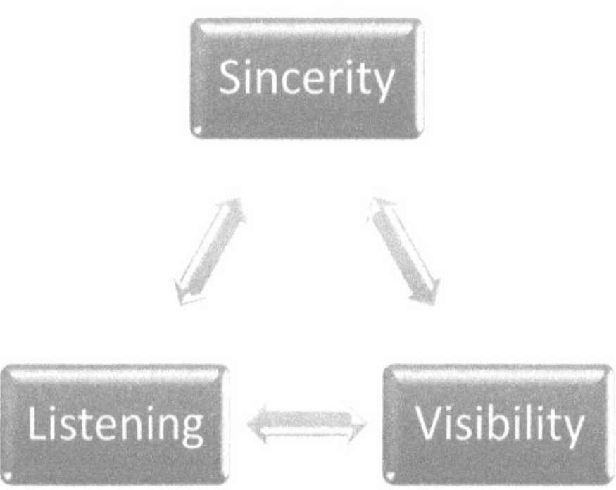

There are three aspects of great communications that need to be kept in mind: *sincerity*, *visibility* and *listening*.

Sincerity and honesty matter a lot. Great leaders do not speak like corporate robots. They speak in their *own* voice. They do not pretend to be someone they are not. *Employees like, respect and follow "real" leaders*. Employees detest false, double-headed, forked-tongue leaders. Genuine leaders *say what they mean* and *mean what they say*. There is no dichotomy between the said words and their meanings. What a pleasure it is to hear such leaders communicate!

Visibility is about being physically present from time-to-time to interact with all stakeholders. Remote communications through emails and phone calls alone are not amenable to great followership among employees. Step into their cubicles or stop by their workstations to chat, share and bond with members of the team. Care must be taken to do this with *all* members of the team irrespective of one's personal likes and dislikes. It must also be ensured that the body language exhibited is genuinely positive, warm and encouraging. One boss had the habit of putting his arm around the shoulder of any particularly demotivated worker or someone who had had a bad day. It almost always brought a smile back on the face of the employee.

Communication is about treating people right and being seen to do that often.

Listening well is the ability to understand another person's perspective or situation clearly and empathetically. Empathy invigorates; sympathy enfeebles. A good leader does not sympathize but empathizes. Active listening is one of the core communication skills of leaders which is under-addressed and needs to be well developed in a good leader.

Exercise

- What is your assessment of your team / department leader or the organization's leader who has communicated with you in the past one year? Tick the appropriate place on the scale below:

  Low Sincerity---------|----------|-----------|----------|-----------|--------High Sincerity

  Low Visibility   -------|----------|-----------|----------|----------|--------High Visibility

  Poor Listening -------|----------|-----------|----------|-----------|--------Good Listening

- What is your assessment of your own communications with your team / department in the past one year? Tick the appropriate place on the scale below:

  Low Sincerity---------|----------|-----------|--------|----------|--------High Sincerity

  Low Visibility   -------|--------|-----------|--------|----------|---------High Visibility

  Poor Listening -------|----------|-----------|--------|---------|--------Good Listening

- If you have received feedback from your team members what area do you feel you need to work on in order to communicate effectively?

  ____

  ____

  ____

  ____

  ____

  ____

The "How" of Good Communications

Communications is a process. It has three sender related activities, one receiver related activity and two system related activities. First, the communicator must be fully conversant with the target receiver – performance, background, motivation level, etc. This helps in the most important part of the process – the encoding.

Encoding

Encoding is where the communicator *creates the message* that is to be delivered. Creating the message requires the following: using the receiver's language, a good understanding of the context of the communication, and a reasonably good understanding of the receptivity level of the receiver.

Transmission

Now that the message has been encoded, it has to be decided how the message should be transmitted. Who should say what has to be said? Often the leader decides to send a spokesperson / substitute especially when bad news has to be conveyed. All those who aspire to be great leaders should deliver, both, the good and the bad news in person. When communication is done in person, a leader basks in reflected glory when it is good news and displays courage when it is bad news.

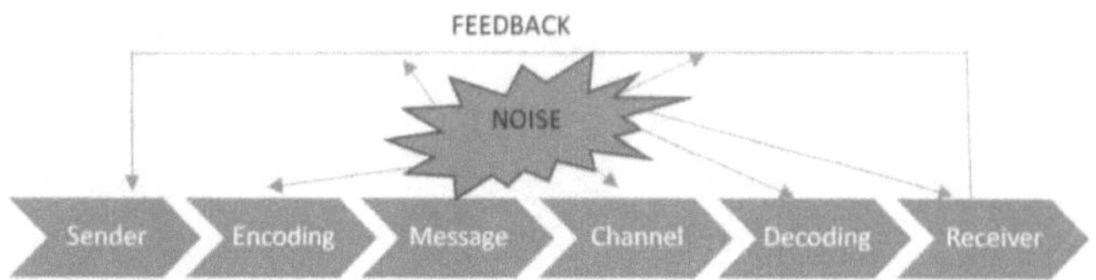

Medium

Third, what medium for communication is ideal? Townhall? Intra-office group messaging platform? Newsletter? Email? Video? It depends on the importance of the message, expected audience, geographical dispersion etc. If it requires interaction and listening to grievances, the townhall format is best owing to its face to face nature and real-time interactivity with a large audience. If the receivers are a group of 10-20 members (like sales teams), a face to face small group discussion is best. If it is geographically spread over a large area, a video conferencing is probably most appropriate. The idea is to communicate the message *in one instance* to all who need to hear it. This prevents the grapevine working overtime and causing widespread distress and confusion with rumours spreading chaos.

Decoding

At the decoding stage, the receiver of the communications is at work. The receiver is checking for relevance, timing, sincerity, the complexity of the message, ease of understanding, call for action or mere information level content. The receiver decides the success of the communication. He or she can hear instead of listening; disregard it for lack of relevance, timing, sincerity, simplicity of language, or call for immediate action. No matter how great the message, if the receiver decides to ignore it, the communicator will never succeed. Leaders must be aware of this reality. Therefore, focus on the receiver must be complete.

Noise

All through this process, there are disruptive cues collectively called "noise". Noise is anything which interferes with the communications process and hinders the receiver from responding in the communicator's intended way. For instance, a very important message being delivered via videoconference may not have the desired impact if connectivity gets repeatedly disrupted. Or, in a townhall meeting, if there is a group of employees heckling or questioning pointlessly, the leader's message might get diluted in smaller whirlpools of discussions.

Exercise

In your experience where have you faced the maximum difficulty while communicating (rank in order of difficulty from 1 being most difficult to 5 being least difficult):

Understanding the receiver

Encoding the message

Choosing the communication media

Noise in the system

Receiver not appreciating the message

AIDA Model of Communication

Communication focuses on 4 broad objectives – Awareness, Interest, Desire, and Action (AIDA). The purpose of any communicator is to take new members through the four steps and keep older members of the team at the 'desire' and 'action' levels. Awareness about the culture and processes of the team and the company are important inputs for new members of a team. As they mature, they go from interest in the workings of the organization to a desire to contribute significantly by taking action aligned with the company's values and goals. This critical job of inducting, training and energizing team members belongs to the leader. One of the authors recollects the time taken by the CEO of the first company he worked for coming to spend three whole days with new Management Trainees in the company. The fact that the CEO of a large company took three working days off to get to know new inductees had a lasting impression of what the company stood for. Awareness, interest, desire and action stages were all covered very well in those three days. All fresh management trainees unanimously agreed that the leader was a class apart.

Given the nature of the communication process, a leader must decide whether it is attention, interest, desire, action, or assurance that is the desired outcome of the communication. Sometimes it is a mix of these objectives that might be the desired outcome. For instance, if a company is being acquired by another, the leader must not only inform existing employees but also assure them of continued employment security. If a team needs to course correct, the leader must inform, create desire and ensure members take action. The goals of communications must be set out clearly in advance and a suitable message must be selected, encoded and communicated via the most optimum channel. Objectives and Key Results (OKRs) of communication must be set clearly for achieving success.

Leaders achieve success with their communication skills when they:

- Communicate regularly
- Listen empathetically
- Keep it simple, straightforward, and sincere
- Use storytelling where necessary
- Back it up with action

Communicating regularly

Essentially this means being visible regularly, sometimes in a direct way and sometimes in a non-obtrusive way. Use all the media channels at one's disposal according to the context. It also involves making sure that communication channels with the team members are always free and without blockages. For instance, if there have not been any inputs from your front line salesmen lately, the leader should wonder why. Is it because the middle layers are speaking for them? Is it because the front line people feel that the leader does not meet them often enough? Is it because someone in the frontline was punished for communicating with the leader directly? The cause must be determined and resolved.

Exercise:

How often does your organization leader communicate with employees? In what ways? Is the frequency good enough, too little or too much?

Who?	How often?	What mediums?	Too little?	Just Right?	Too often?
Example: CEO	Once a month	Newsletter, townhalls, mails		Yes	
Your immediate leader:					
Your CEO					

How often do you communicate with your team? Is it as per a schedule? Or as and when needed only? Is it only through one or two methods?

Who?	How often?	What mediums?	Too little?	Just Right?	Too often?
You as a leader:					

Listening empathetically

Listening empathetically involves respecting and appreciating team members. It does not mean agreeing with everything that comes from the audience, but agreeing to disagree respectfully. One employee in middle management in an organization wrote to the leader of the organization about some changes that would be good for the organization as a whole. The leader's response was more a 'retort' than an empathetic reply. A retort is a response that is designed to snub or end the discussion abruptly. Instead, if the response had been based on empathetic listening, there could have been a healthy, fruitful discussion. A communicator who bulldozes alternative views is only able to do so because of his power or position of authority. That is *not* the kind of leader who communicates well. He or she does not achieve buy-in from the team members.

An effective way of being an empathetic listener is to create the right situation for proper communication – no phones, no people coming and going into the room, and a pre-decided time for the communication; the opportunity to ask many questions for clarifications and validation; use of the LSF (Listen-Summarize-Paraphrase) technique to help the other person know that you are actually listening to him or her, not just hearing; and finally allowing silent moments to let the communication sink in and be fully grasped.

Exercise

Evaluate the last three communication events you have had (one with a senior, one with a peer, and one with a junior).

Scoring:

If you get 3 'Yes'es, it is a moderately good situation. If you get 4 'Yes'es it is a fairly good situation. And if you get 5 'Yes'es then you are definitely in a very good communication situation.

3 persons you last communicated with on something important	Was rapport created by making the ambience comfortable?	Was there any observation of the emotional tone of the conversation	Were many questions asked in the form of a dialogue?	Was there any LSF?	Was there silence from time to time to let the discussion sink in?
Example: DGM (Ops)	No	Yes	Yes	No	No
1.					
2.					
3.					

Based on your last three communication interactions (as above), what would you like to focus on to be an empathetic listener?

____

____

____

____

____

____

KISSS

Keeping the message simple, straightforward and sincere is easily done when the intent is honest. Leaders who communicate in a long-winded, meandering way often do so due to insincerity. Leaders with good communication skills talk straight and with respect. Listeners 'feel' the genuineness of the message. Many African-Americans have this wonderful way of saying they understand what someone is trying to communicate. They say, "I feel you". In effect, what they are saying is, "I understand you with my heart". KISSS brings buy-in from the team and from the organization. Without buy-in the message falls like water on a duck's back without the desired impact.

Exercise: (tick one)

1. Usually how long are your communications when you send an email:
   a.   *3 lines*
   b.   *5 lines*
   c.   *> 10 lines*
2. Usually, how long are your talks with your team members?
   a.   5-10 minutes
   b.   10-30 minutes
   c.   > 30 minutes
3. How often have team members come back seeking clarifications?
   a. After every talk, because I encourage discussion in the group
   b. Once in a while as I am usually very clear in my communications
   c. Never! I am always very clear what I want to say

Email communication is best between 3-5 lines. Whatever important content that has to be said can be said in those many lines. Besides, employees do not like to read lengthy emails. They have work to do.

Talks should be precise and rarely exceed 5-10 minutes by a leader. Rest should be Q&A, discussions, clarifications, etc. Anything beyond this limit creates boredom.

Communication meetings should have start and end timings clearly mentioned.

If team members come back seeking clarification after almost every talk, then the communication may not have been simple, straightforward and sincere. If they never come back, it might be a sign that there is no open culture to discuss things rather than clarity in communication on the leader's part. Be cautious.

Storytelling: It is an irresistible tool for capturing the listener's imagination. Most of us remember the stories from all the speeches we have heard more than the actual content of the communication. Which means that if the message can be transformed into a story and then communicated, it would have a higher impact and retention. People are attracted to stories because of our social nature. Storytelling also releases cortisol when tense moments in the story appear and the feel-good chemical oxytocin when there is a release or empathy moment in the story. For example, the news that a key member of the team is leaving the organization can be crippling. But what if a story of how the organization was instrumental in the person's growth as well as how the individual contributed to the growth of the organization can be spun in an interesting way? It would take the sting out of the departure. If a few words can be said on how the best practices of the organization would be carried forward to the organization the individual is going to join, it would give a sense of continuity of the organization's legacy. Hence, instead of merely looking at the loss from an organization's point of view, it could be looked at as the organization's gift to the industry! That would be storytelling.

Storytelling is most effective when it uses Freytag's Pyramid of Storytelling:

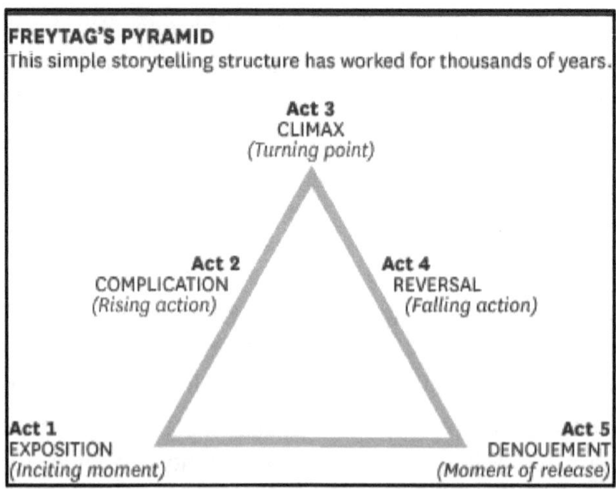

Source: HBR, March 2014

Take a look at the Budweiser Puppy Love commercial at the Super Bowl and the power of storytelling using the Freytag Pyramid becomes clear. A leader needs to build his or her communication in the same way wherever possible.

Exercise

In a business situation when the team is fighting for sales, market share, topline, bottomline, new products, profitability and distributors, is there any room for storytelling? Where?

____

____

____

____

____

____

Here's an example of the storytelling skills of Moe Levine, a great trial lawyer in the U.S.

Widely recognized as the leading trial lawyer of his time, Moe Levine often used the "whole man" theory to successfully influence juries to empathize with his clients.

Seeking compensation for a client who had lost both arms in an accident, Levine surprised the court and jury, who were accustomed to long closing arguments, by painting a brief and emotionally devastating picture instead:

He said to the jury, "As you know, about an hour ago we broke for lunch. I saw the bailiff come and take you all as a group to have lunch in the jury room. Then I saw the defense attorney, Mr. Horowitz. He and his client decided to go to lunch together. So, I turned to my client, Harold, and said: "Why don't you and I go to lunch together?" We went across the street to that little restaurant and had lunch. *(Significant pause)*. Ladies and gentlemen, I just had lunch with my client. He has no arms. He has to eat like a dog. Thank you very much."

Levine reportedly won one of the largest settlements in the history of the state of New York.

Source: Harrison Monarth, Harvard Business Review, March 2014.

Back it up with action: As described in earlier chapters, leaders have to "walk the talk". At some point, words alone will not be sufficient even if they are very powerful. Action brings credibility and gives birth to trust. Leaders who only talk, lose both quickly. Action is an expression of commitment to the spoken word. True to the old saying, "Action speaks louder than words", a leader with good communication skills must have the courage and conviction to do something about what he or she speaks or promises or encourages. Don't be a leader nicknamed "hot air", or "empty bag", or "all bark no bite".

"Do as I say, not as I do" might have worked in earlier times. Now it is more, "Do as I do, whatever I might say." Leaders who are action-oriented must also balance their people skills. Walking the talk involves the leader helping people achieve their goals, giving them freedom and autonomy, ferociously defending the company's values, improving the lives of one's team members, and listening more than talking, just as much as focusing on number crunching and overcoming competitors.

People feel

As a leader, what you make your employees *feel* will always stay with them long after what you said and did are forgotten. You can talk the talk, but can you walk the walk? If there is an aspiration to be a great leader, then one must master this principle.

In the business of politics, Mahatma Gandhi walked the walk with such regularity that ordinary followers found it tough to keep up. Uncompromising and steadfast, Gandhi was also a people's person, caring, listening, empathizing, and leading. His leadership gave the world a model moral code.

Action in leadership sometimes brings forth enemies. Tough actions make people feel upset and sometimes turn them into mortal enemies. Leadership brings loneliness. One must learn how to cope with that. Sometimes your followers backstab you. Then as a leader, you will feel let down and worthless. One must find the courage to go on in both situations.

Exercise:

How many times in the last six months have you, as a leader, walked the talk? Give an example.

____

____

____

____

____

How many times in the last six months have you, as a leader, not walked the talk? Example?

____

____

____

____

____

What factors would you ascribe your inability to walk your talk?

____

____

____

____

____

How have inhibiting circumstances affected your relationship with your team?

____

____

____

____

To avoid failure in walking your talk, take care to observe the following 5 steps:

1. Be careful what you claim or promise (under-promise and over-deliver).
2. Ensure you have Plan B ready (in case Plan A fails).
3. Monitor your walk carefully and regularly (to align with your talk).
4. Make it a habit to talk wisely and thoughtfully (so that your talk is not impulsive).
5. Take inputs and buy-in from your team for your talk (so that the walk is not yours alone).

Body Language

No discussion on communications can be complete without a look at the importance of body language. It is interesting to note that according to research, almost 70% of understanding of a personal one-on-one communication comes from non-verbal cues. Signals such as tone of voice, posture, smile, crossed arms and legs, leaning in or pushing back, fidgetiness or calmness are all important in understanding the communicator and the message.

Body language is the conscious and unconscious movements and postures by which attitudes and feelings are communicated. These unspoken elements of communication convey true feelings and emotions. A leader must be good at reading these signs and conveying communication with the proper body language.

Difficult conversations are an uncomfortable part of life at work. Dealing with your team members about poor performance or goal non-accomplishment can be tough. Having to let go of a team member can be devastating for both. There is often a lot of defensiveness and bruised egos and even anger. And these emotions if not read properly lead to confrontations rather than productive communication.

Certain cues of difficult conversation situations are as follows:

Arms folded in front of the body (not open to you or your message, defensive, closed-minded)

Tense facial expression (nervous, afraid, dangerous, angry, distrustful)

Body facing away from you (indifference, casualness, non-serious, defensive, evasive)

Eyes looking down, minimal eye contact (timid, untruthful, lacking confidence)

Certain cues of unengaged audiences are as follows:

Sitting slumped, eyes focused elsewhere (low involvement, low engagement)

Fidgeting, fiddling with pens, clothes, buttons, and phones (low engagement)

Scribbling, doodling, looking at the time often (distracted, engaged in other thoughts, boredom)

Certain cues of an aggressive audience or communicator are as follows:

Hands on hips, chest out, legs apart (aggression, dominating, dismissive)

Glaring eyes, heavy breathing, stammering (excited, angry, maybe furious, offensive)

Barely touching handshake / crushing handshake (dismissive, showing power)

Body language is a language worth learning for leaders who want to communicate empathetically. It is important for leaders to understand when to be assertive and when to be soft. Knowledge of body language sets us free from the mistakes that can occur by depending solely on spoken words.

Leaders should also be aware that the spoken word and associated body language should match. For instance, offering praise to an individual while looking away from the person will be understood as false praise.

One can train one's body to talk a certain language but insincerity and dishonesty will expose you in an unguarded moment. For instance, a firm handshake and a straight look into the eyes might give the impression of a confident person but when a challenge is thrown up out of the blue and the individual's training does not get time to get activated, then the true self will appear, however briefly. That is a giveaway. Nevertheless, good body language training triggers behavioural change. When you are trained to *look* confident, often you actually end up *being* confident. When you train yourself to *appear* open and warm, usually it results in you *becoming* open and warm. So practice regularly, correctly and sincerely.

Reading other people's body language as well as writing and speaking your own positive body language are important steps on the road to being an effective leader. Find a coach if you have to. Invest in it. Master it.

If you want to do it on your own, record yourself on video, talking in a formal situation. Check for gaps, aahs, ticks (like constantly touching your nose or your hair), posture, tone of voice, modulation of voice. Now compare it to a few good speakers you admire. Keep a logbook of your improvement journey by recording your speeches or talks using a phone camera on a tripod. It could look something like this:

Session	Date	Duration (min:sec)	Flaws	Strengths
Session 1	1/1/2020	5:12	17 aahs; 3 face touches; 6 fidgetings with the watch; voice totally monotonous; limp hand gestures; low passion	Good content
Session 2				
Session 3				
Session 4....				
....				
Session n				

Exercise

You are giving a motivational talk to your team after a month of low sales. Of the thirteen members in your team, two sitting next to each other are alert and upright, looking at their smart phones every few minutes. One of the two gets a call and steps out after excusing himself. Your talk continues. Some of the others are sitting downcast, looking at their shoes. One team member in particular has not looked up even once. A few in the front are sitting up and listening intently. The person who got the phone call comes back in. As he sits down he leans back in his chair with his legs stretched out in front of him. A brief glance is exchanged between him and his partner. You ask him about his sales performance and he offers a casual answer looking away from you at the others in the team with a half-smile. Meeting gets over. Discussions get stretched over tea. On the 31st of the month you get two resignation letters. Whose are they? How do you know?

Lead from the back and let others believe they are in front

Mandela loved to reminisce about his boyhood and his lazy afternoons herding cattle. "You know," he would say, "you can only lead them from behind." He would then raise his eyebrows to make sure I got the analogy.

As a boy, Mandela was greatly influenced by Jongintaba, the tribal king who raised him. When Jongintaba had meetings of his court, the men gathered in a circle, and only after all had spoken did the king speak. "The chief's job," Mandela said, "was not to tell people what to do but to form a consensus. "Don't enter the debate too early," he used to say."

During the time I worked with Mandela, he often called meetings of his kitchen cabinet at his home in Houghton, a lovely old suburb of Johannesburg. He would gather half a dozen men, Ramaphosa, Thabo Mbeki, and others around the dining-room table or sometimes in a circle in his driveway. Some of his colleagues would shout at him — to move faster, to be more radical — and Mandela would simply listen. When he finally did speak at those meetings, he slowly and methodically summarized everyone's points of view and then unfurled his own thoughts, subtly steering the decision in the direction he wanted without imposing it. The trick of leadership is allowing yourself to be led too. "It is wise," he said, "to persuade people to do things and make them think it was their own idea."

From:

Mandela: His 8 Lessons of Leadership

By Richard Stengel Wednesday, July 09, 2008

Key learnings from this chapter for you:

1.

2.

3.

4.

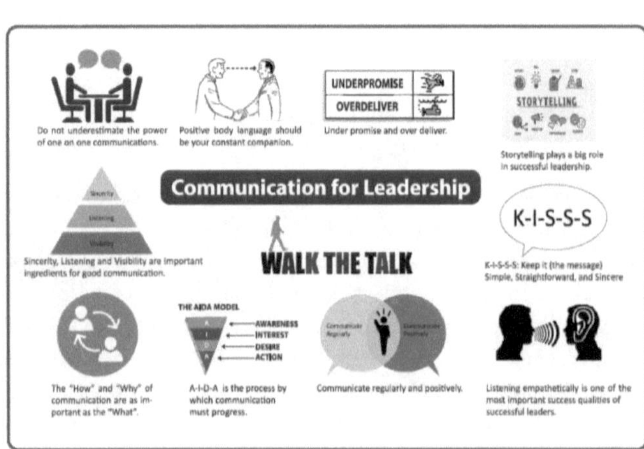

LEADERSHIP ESSENTIAL # 7
HANDLING FAILURES

Failures are a part and parcel of human endeavour. Most people experience more failures than successes. Leaders have to tilt the balance in favour of more successes to earn and maintain their leadership positions. Even then, as some failures are almost inevitable, it is important that existing and aspiring leaders know how to handle them.

What is Failure?

Failure has many definitions. According to the Cambridge English dictionary, failure is—

a) the fact of someone or something not succeeding

(eg. *The negotiations were a complete failure*)

b) the fact of not doing something that you must do or are expected to do

(eg. *Her failure to see the market signals resulted in the demise of the company*)

c) the fact of something not working, or stopping working as well as it should.

(eg. *The number of CEOs quitting last year due to business failures has risen sharply*)

Main causes of failure

Failures in corporations could result due to various reasons. The two most important ones for leaders to be aware of and manage are:

a) change management failure

b) innovation management failure

Change management failures result from the inability of putting transformation items in a culturally acceptable manner. For example, if the leader of a large legacy telecom company like BSNL is unable to install and lead cultural change for employees to become more agile and customer-centric, it can lead to loss of customer relevance due to change management failure. Leaders trying to change corporate culture are likely to face this kind of failure. A good illustration of this type of failure is the case of Air India. Many leaders have attempted to set things right culturally at the national flag carrier but have not succeeded.

Innovation management failures result from the failure to create a robust innovation strategy and the failure to evolve with the market. Examples of innovation failures are numerous and have been well documented. Kodak failing to adapt itself for the digital onslaught despite being the first in the world to actually invent digital photography led to its downfall from the pre-eminent position in imaging products it had held for many decades. IBM, Nokia, Blockbuster, and JVC are other examples of innovation management failures.

Focus on People, Process and Innovation: It can help avoid failures

Leaders in the 21st-century corporations would do well to adopt a *flexible* leadership model with an emphasis on people, process and innovation.

It is important to note that the first of the three things to focus on for successful leadership is "people". Without good quality, highly motivated "people", no leader can deliver consistently over a long period. The premium Ritz Carlton hotel chain is an excellent example of highly motivated staff fulfilling the leadership's vision. Every employee at the Ritz from housekeeping to management has a no-questions-asked pre-approved sanction to spend up to $2000 (yes, Rs. 1,40,000! Simply wow!) on any hotel guest in order to give excellent customer service. Their motto "*We are ladies and gentlemen serving ladies and gentlemen*' embodies respect for their employees first which in turn creates respect for their guests. That is an awesome approach to get your people excited, engaged and enthused!

Exercise

Have you ever tried offering respect to your team first before anything else? If yes, how did you benefit as a leader?

____

____

____

____

The second emphasis must be on mastery over processes within the organization. Many companies have discovered the benefits of the Japanese way of *"Kaizen"* – continuous improvement of processes by asking the why, what, when, where, who and how questions. A leader's role requires that the focus on process change management must be done in a minimally disruptive manner, or, if disruption cannot be avoided, then the team must be informed and taken into confidence. You will be surprised at the level of buy-in that can be achieved from employees when things are discussed and debated. The effects are often magical. Of course, there will be dissent but effective leaders need to anticipate and offset dissent, respectfully. What does USA, Burma and Liberia have in common? They are the only three countries in the world which have not adopted the metric system (where speedometers read mph; weight is measured in pounds and temperature is recorded in degrees Fahrenheit). US President Jimmy Carter's administration in 1975 tried to implement the metric system. In the face of complete apathy from the public at large, the plan was shelved in 1982. Lesson? Culture eats process for lunch. Prescription: understand organizational culture well and then align process changes to leverage that culture.

Exercise

Have you ever launched a process change in your organization and met with a strong pushback because of cultural issues? Briefly describe what happened. Did you consider your organization / team's cultural barriers?

____

____

____

____

____

____

____

The third emphasis is managing innovation as a strategic element for organizational success. Failure to do so results in leadership failure. McDonald's "Made for You" – a customized food creation process for its customers — was an 'innovation' failure as it took away from efficiency and reliability. McDonald's is a place where people go for quick and consistent fast food with short wait times. "Made for You" put more emphasis on trying to be something which they were not supposed to be — Made to Order and long queues. If the leadership had taken the time to seek out feedback and tested the innovation concept before rolling it out, a disaster might have been prevented.

Great leaders work on all three aspects of avoiding failure and embracing business success. As can be appreciated from the above, failures can occur (or avoided) anywhere, anytime.

Exercise

In the last 6 months examine your leadership as per the grid below (one example has been given for you to fill in the rest):

Area of Leadership Failure	People	Process	Innovation	Reason for leadership failure
Go to market plan for a new shampoo	Channel partners not supportive	Channel needs to see the benefit in it for themselves	Five-in-one shampoo	Inability to inspire sales team and channel partners about the potential of the product

Before we get to handling failures, it is necessary to dig into some additional causes of leadership failure in organizations. Here are some of them:

1. Taking the business in the **wrong strategic direction**. For example, when Netflix split into separately paid services, it was a wrong strategic decision for the company which had earlier revolutionized the video industry. Similarly, Kingfisher Airlines became shaky the day it acquired the no-frills airline Air Deccan (among other things). Wrong choices, wrong roads, wrong outcomes.

2. Allowing **factors other than merit** to be employed for choosing leaders. For example, at a once very successful North American smartphone maker, nepotism played some role in poor succession planning. In Indian PSUs the iron law till recently was that seniority trumped merit in most cases. Family-based business houses have had its share of problems in accession to top spots for family outsiders.

3. **Corruption:** When leadership is or becomes corrupted there is only one way for the organization – downwards. Enron is the perfect example. After hiding fraud for many years, the leadership finally found itself in prison. In India, the leadership at a leading Indian private bank got compromised with organizational interests becoming subservient to the Chief Executive's personal interests.

4. Ineptitude or **lack of ability to lead**: This is a major reason why leaders fail – being chosen for a profile they are inherently incapable of fulfilling. An American banking and financial products supermarket (one of the largest in the world at the time) in the 2000s committed the mistake of appointing a leader who committed a series of missteps leading finally to his ouster. At one of India's largest legacy corporate houses, the new CEO's inability to carry the Trust members with him resulted in his ignominious ouster. The ability to lead is not in every leader who gets into the driving seat.

5. **Insincerity and Dishonesty**: This is not only exhibited in the handling of business operations but also in terms of unsavoury dealings with the opposite gender. It also refers to dual standards for top management and lower-level employees in treating reported cases of unacceptable financial, illegal or immoral behaviour. Uber, Google and TERI are some companies whose

leaders failed by bringing disrepute to their companies and their employees.

Organizations go through immense turmoil when their leaders are unable to lead well and with honesty. 20,000 employees walked out at Google when they felt their leaders were not up to the mark in terms of dealing with sexual harassment complaints or kowtowing to China in undermining the very idea of "free and unbiased search".

Exercise

1. In your current organization or any previous ones (without naming them), did you feel that your leader(s) let you and the company down? If yes, how?

____

____

____

____

2. Did anybody raise the issue? What happened thereafter?

____

____

____

3. What would you have liked to be done differently?

____

____

____

4. Have you ever faced a situation as a leader when someone came up and said that your leadership is below expectations (in nicer words)?

____

____

____

____

Why do leadership disasters occur?

1. *The Power Distance:* One of the prime reasons for leadership failures lies in a characteristic of many collectivist, hierarchical societies (like Indian, Korean and Japanese) – the power distance. We do not like to point out the failures of our seniors and leaders. We consider it disrespectful and 'not our place' to point out the mistakes of elders or leaders. We prefer to suffer it quietly rather than tell our leaders, managers and elders that they are making a mistake. In turn, this leads to failures of the leader and the system.

2. *Fear in the system*: Fear of repercussions for stating the truth is very real in many cultures which permeates the business environment. Not agreeing with the boss or leader is counted as being anti-system. Resisting unethical demands often result in penalization. Women employees and subordinates know this the best. Creating a fear-free environment is the key solution.

3. *Wrong selection process*: Too much emphasis on experience kills the creative aspect of leadership. Psychometric testing for *interest* in leadership roles rather than the *ability* to lead is another wrong approach in leadership selection. A third wrong approach is too much "people empathy" and too little "task orientation". Leaders who do not maintain a balance between the two often end up failing to lead. Too often,

a leader once instated in the position wants to sail quietly without rocking the boat at all. This causes disasters too.

4. *Poor early warning systems*: Often leaders out of a sense of insecurity surround themselves with people who are inferior to them. Such a circle is often filled with sycophants and yes-men. Their mission in life is to camouflage looming disaster signs and keep feeding the leader only rosy pictures. Lulled into a sense of false superstardom, such leaders sink without a trace. A robust and healthy critiquing system is what good leadership should strive for.

5. *Sense of arrogance*: Often when a leader tastes a little success, there creeps in a sense of arrogance. Arrogance is defined as (among other things) a "sense of false superiority". This results in discounting the suggestions of others. One expression which captures this tendency well is "my way or the highway". Arrogance makes a leader impervious to good advice. Such leaders think they have it all figured out. Soon the good people in the team start moving out and there are only those left who survive on loyalty and sycophancy.

6. *Inability to see the dynamic future*: Changes are happening at breakneck speed in the business and technology fields. Leaders who do not see the future changing on the horizon and sit pretty on their past laurels, suffer catastrophes. Sometimes such leaders are responsible for entire companies folding up. Leaders without vision take the company backwards or, in the worst-case scenario, into extinction.

7. *Failure to manage top-level interpersonal dynamics*: Often many organizations are rife with negative "politics". The term is used negatively here to express all that is wrong with group dynamics in the

organization. At the heart of such negativity is the hunger for power. Since that cannot be eliminated, a leader must be able to navigate the choppy waters carefully and with authority. Inability to assert authority leads to alternative power centres cropping up which undermine the leader's position.

Exercise

1. Have you observed any of the above 7 reasons for leadership failure? Please explain briefly.

2. What was the impact of the leader's failure on the company/division/team?

3. Have you ever personally faced failure because of any of the above 7 reasons? If yes, which reason(s) was evident in your situation?

4. What was the impact of your failure on your team? Be honest!

____

____

____

____

____

5. Do you think there could be any other major reason for the failure of a leader? If yes, what?

____

____

____

____

____

What to do when faced with failure as a Leader?

Leaders have some options when they sense failure looming ahead. For one, they can brace it out boldly by accepting the mistake made, evaluating one's situation objectively, talking to trustworthy people, learning from the situation one is in, and moving forward. The other option is to deny the mistake, blame others for the mess one is in, create bad blood within the team, and stagnate. The choice is yours.

All of us have different ways of coping with failure or loss.

Some become aggressive and vindictive. Some blame others for their failure. Some withdraw into a shell and others might resign and move on unable to bear the humiliation.

The fallouts of any of the above are that it can make a bad situation worse. Resigning and leaving the organization might haunt one forever.

Blaming others for your failures would be churlish, childish and immature showing a low emotional quotient.

Becoming aggressive and vindictive might lead to a revolt from team members who now have you on the back foot.

All the above paths can lead to deeply negative outcomes for the organization, team members and yourself.

What is called for is a mature approach. The mature approach entails taking a step back and reflecting on what actually happened and assessing the situation dispassionately. It is a good practice to have a mentor with whom you can discuss your failure (and successes) for fair and balanced feedback.

A dispassionate assessment of failure requires the following **"12 Steps of Failure Management"**:

1. Understanding and accepting that a failure has happened. Denial is of no use.
2. Revisiting the parameters that had been set. Were they realistic and doable?
3. Which factors played a major role in the failure?
4. Was it possible to have had control over those factors?
5. If not, then was it a complete failure?
6. If yes, what are the reasons you were not able to see the signals?
7. What needs to be corrected? Can it be done? If yes, what steps?
8. If not, is there a need to change the goalposts, set new targets?
9. After the assessment, bring the team into a town hall session and share your analysis.
10. Discuss learnings from your failure and set new goal(s) with the team.

11. If people within your team caused you to fail, two options: counsel and keep; inform and fire
12. Inform management (or board) of your analysis and seek support.

The above 12 steps of Failure Management, if adopted, would not only show you in a positive light but also one with an analytical bent of mind. You would be perceived as a structured person, mature in your outlook, dispassionate in your examination of the causes of your failure, brave enough to brace the discussion with your team, inclusive enough to involve them to achieve new goals and smart enough to discuss with your superiors the way ahead.

The hallmark of a successful leader is to have the intelligence to know when (s)he has failed and the wisdom to know that s/he can live to fight another day.

Failure is a learning process. People often don't think about it that way, especially if they've been successful in life. However, failure can be just as valuable as success. Instead of decreasing your confidence and your feelings about your abilities, it should boost those. Such experiences make you a better leader.

Also, stop beating yourself up about failure. Overcome the tendency to blame yourself beyond a certain point. Stop dwelling on the past and look at the future. Stop getting entangled in a psychological web of self-pity and blaming others.

Exercise

1. When faced with a failure in your organization, what have you seen your leader(s) do?

____

____

____

____

____

2. If you are faced with a failure in your job, what do you normally do?

____

____

____

____

____

3. Would following the 12 steps of Failure Management help you in your leadership position in case of a failure? Why or why not?

____

____

____

____

____

Important Note on Failures

Failures are milestones on one's way to success. There is not a single person in the history of our species who has not failed. Some fail more than others. The real trick is to keep going. Ask yourself if there is any other way to deal with failure – except to get up, dust yourself and move on? Would you rather give up, lie on your back in self-pity, blaming others and drown in your own sea of negative thoughts? Or not? Find your purpose and keep moving with the final objective in your sight. You have a task to achieve *irrespective* of your failures. Actually, because of your failures you learn that life is worth living and that goals are worth achieving. You have got to prove it to yourself that you can do it, if not for anybody else.

An Anecdote of Leadership Failure Management

There is a very long list of failures who finally made it to great heights. From Abraham Lincoln to Dhirubhai Ambani and Katy Perry to Sunil Bharti Mittal, there are numerous stories in every field where *overnight success* was often *many years* in the making. Stories of indomitable courage in business, sports, entertainment, music, science and literature are inspirational. It tells us the power of not giving up. One such story is that of Ratan Tata, erstwhile head of TATA Sons, the holding trust of the $100 billion dollar Tata Conglomerate.

Heralded as one of the greatest industrialists of modern India, Ratan Naval Tata, faced failures and tough times in many situations. His first major failure was in trying to turn around Empress Mills in Mumbai in 1977. He faced stiff resistance from militant trade union leader, Datta Samant, which he could not resolve. Eventually, the Mills had to be shut down. Then, he spent his initial years after taking over from JRD Tata at Bombay House trying to rein in the satraps who had been allowed full freedom by his uncle JRD. It took him a long time to assert his authority over these individual company heads. Russi Mody and Ajit Kerkar openly fought with Ratan Tata after the latter was nominated as Chairman, jumping over the heads of Mody (TISCO), Darbari Seth (Tata Tea), Ajit Kerkar (Indian

Hotels) and Nani Palkhivala (Board Member). Ratan Tata had to navigate this extremely hostile climate created by the independent heads. Mody had to be ousted based on irregularities in the appointment of certain key top functionaries at TISCO. Seth and Kerkar were eased out by Tata after he brought in a new "70 years cut-off age for MDs". Therefore, though he belonged to the family, Ratan Tata had to prove his mettle at every step. He did this by careful engineering in order to steer the Tata Conglomerate into the new business environment post 1991. He kept on forging ahead despite repeated failures and temporary setbacks.

The Role of a Mentor in times of Failure

A mentor is an experienced and trusted adviser. A mentor's experience helps because he has "been there, done that". A mentor you trust is helpful because you can share details without having to hide facts or pretend in order to maintain your self-esteem. A mentor should be chosen carefully. Some qualities in a prospective mentor: values in alignment with your own, capable and willing to give honest feedback, loads of experience, humility, confidentiality, helpfulness, wisdom and vision.

The mentor is one who understands you well, listens actively and empathetically, gives you scathing feedback if need be, connects you to his or her network, and encourages you through the tough times. For at least two senior leaders the authors know personally, their mentor is their spouse. It has worked for them. Others prefer to pick a mentor from industry. The mentor can be a perfect bouncing board for overcoming failure.

When you become a Mentor for a Failed Leader / Team Member

After a successful tenure as a leader, there will be times when your team members would seek you out for mentorship. What are the signals? Often a team member comes to discuss issues, ideas and strategy with you. Ensure that he / she is not short-circuiting any line of control. And then be miserly in providing advice at first. This is to make sure that he / she is not seeking your advice only to get closer to you for various professional reasons. Once he / she starts implementing your initial suggestions, you might want to test the person again. After you are convinced about the genuineness of the person's interest, only then should you step into a full-fledged mentoring role.

Exercise

1. Have you sought out a mentor yet? If not, why?

   ____

   ____

   ____

   ____

2. If you have a mentor, what have you benefited from that person?

   ____

   ____

   ____

   ____

3. Have you mentored a failed team member / leader? If not, why?

____

____

____

____

4. If yes, what would that mentee of yours say about your mentoring style?

____

____

____

____

5. What part about mentoring would you like to change in your mentor?

____

____

____

____

6. What would you like to change in yourself as a mentor of failed team members?

____

____

____

____

Key learnings from this chapter for you:

1.

2.

3.

4.

Failure is an Essential Part of Leadership Success

Dean Kamen, the inventor of Segway, says, "Most people go through life trying to avoid failure. Those who end up doing something are the ones who get up after every failure and keep going. Often their failures are so monumental that they lose all hope. Finally, when they make it, people compliment them. The compliments only come when the failed person succeeds. The important thing is to keep going at it and to remember that failure is a lonely affair and that success, when achieved, becomes the celebratory event. What people forget is that failure is an integral part of a successful leadership journey."

Leadership success depends a lot on seeing problems differently from everybody else and finding solutions that nobody else thinks of. Like inventors, leaders must step up from failures in order to improve the trajectory of the businesses they handle and of the people they lead.

Handling Failure

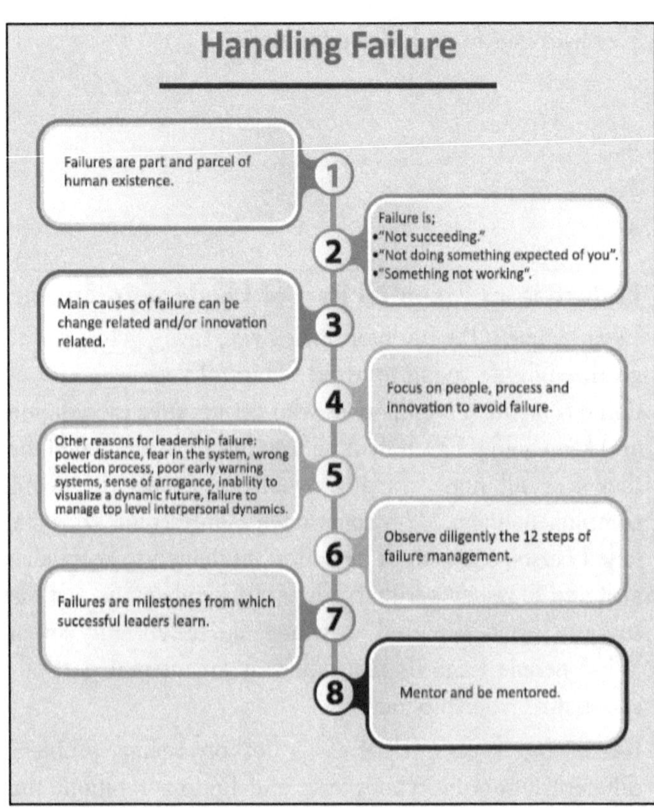

LEADERSHIP ESSENTIAL # 8
CELEBRATING SUCCESS

A Leader's Role

Today, celebrating success is a big part of most organizations — small or big, startups or established, across industry sectors, including not-for-profits. The system takes care of recognition and rewards for outstanding performers and milestones achieved by employees. Automation has crept into much of the celebration of birthdays, anniversaries, tenure milestones and promotions related events. Impersonal e-cards and templated greetings have killed the fun in celebrating successes.

If celebrations and recognitions are taken care of by the organization's HR department or automated software, what is the role of a leader in this case? Apparently, a very important role.

Leaders create a culture in the organization which recognizes challenges of the journey and celebrates milestones so that the team is kept motivated and approaches the next task or milestone with sustained focus and vigour. Leaders must create a culture of giving equal weightage to the journey as well as the end goal.

Appreciation dissolves over time

You might ask when employees are recruited and on-boarded, aren't they screened for self-motivation? Of course, they are. But no matter who it is, everyone has phases of low energy. It is the leader's role to identify the signals and intervene. Since leadership is in the "people business" and people by their very nature can never be consistently upbeat and highly motivated, it is essential for leaders to be people-sensitive. Appreciation must be offered frequently and sincerely to employees. It has been proven by many researchers that appreciation has a bigger and longer impact than monetary rewards alone. At the same time, appreciation has a dissolvable quality. Hence, it needs to be refreshed from time to time.

Once a wife declared in utter frustration to her husband of thirty years that she had not heard the words "I love you" from him for many years. The husband thought for a moment and nonchalantly replied that he had said it when they had married three decades ago. As there was no change in that emotion for him, he did not think it important to mention it ever again. Relationships on the personal front or in the organization do not work like that. We are humans. Humans need constant reinforcement and reassurance. Be free and generous with celebrating small or big successes of your team.

Being task and people-oriented

The leader has eyes on the ultimate goal because it is imperative that things keep moving ahead. Momentum must be kept high to reach the next assignment, *en route* to the end goal. Therefore, remembering to celebrate small moments which are important to the team members is a tough task for the leader. Besides, most leaders got to where they are because they were task-oriented. Now to suddenly ask them to become task *and* people-oriented becomes very difficult. However, good leaders recognize that celebrating success after every unit of achievement motivates and adds momentum to the team which propels them toward the next milestone. Connecting with people in the organization should be a skill that must feature prominently to be a high impact leader.

Catch people doing right

We have been numbed into believing that numbers are the only thing that matters for a leader to deliver. Undoubtedly, numbers are concrete, they are undeniable and they most often win against an abstract, disputable entity such as leader-employee relationship. It is important to understand that leadership is not only in the numbers achieved (though it is an important part), but also the quality of work and the consistent habit of getting things done. The celebration is a day-to-day affair, as a good leader tries to *'catch them doing things right'*. Too many leaders focus on the reverse, trying to catch people committing mistakes. A focus on 'catching people doing things right' will change the work environment dramatically, as team members will know that every good piece of work is noticed and appreciated, which boosts the morale of the team.

When one feels valued at the work place, self-esteem of the team members goes high, and this creates more positivity in the work place. Sharing and celebrating successes strengthen the team.

Contrary to a common practice these days, instead of sharing successes of team members over closed social media groups consisting only of team members, it is the responsibility of the leader to ensure that there are sufficient success stories frequently floating around openly in all media. The above is challenging for a task oriented leader, but is an absolute necessity. One organization even has a "Celebration Bell" where all employees gather to celebrate every achievement of the past month of every employee – doorman to CEO.

Ensuring frequent success stories

How can we ensure that there are frequent success stories?

Our experience of coaxing out success stories in the many companies we worked for have taught us that it works almost every time irrespective of whether you are a front line sales manager or a Director in a company. Occasional low sales and low morale are realities of every organization. Achieving success every day or week or month is difficult.

The first step is to pick your 'A' team members who have the highest success probability.

The second step is to make a detailed action plan for a set of customers who can contribute to your sales in a short period of time; in other words, identify the low hanging fruits, make an attack plan and prepare the sales commandos.

Thirdly, leverage the 'A' team members' customer contacts.

In step four, augment the current relationship with your support and resource it adequately. Follow up with the customer and the team members on a personal basis until the first signs of success start emerging.

Step five is to share successes which will encourage others to look for ways to succeed; then work towards that goal with more focus and determination.

In other words, a leader has to engineer the creation of successes. Further, the language of success-sharing needs to be subtle, not at all boastful and not in a way to put others down. It should never be a comparison exercise between team members. A typical communique could go like this:

"I would like to congratulate Sumitra on a job well done in generating the first Purchase Order for the month from Saturn Pharmaceuticals, a very important customer. Her consistent efforts and focus for the last one month have got her this breakthrough. I am confident that we will hear more success stories from Sumitra and all the other team members".

You might want to go a step further in some cases. *"I would request Sumitra to share with the team how she got this breakthrough at an open house session tomorrow at 11:00 A.M"*.

Sharing of good practices is a cross-learning platform. If the platform is well-designed and transparent, each team member would step forward to share their success mantras.

Such success sharing triggers an appreciative climate among peers, and each congratulatory message is a motivator.

I used to have a mailer series: *"No success is too small to share"*, which gave the team members a platform to share successes irrespective of the sales order size.

Each success is like a building block towards achieving the ultimate quarterly or yearly number. *Hence, the importance of celebrating small milestones each time over.*

Cumulatively, sharing success becomes a matter of *pride* as each and every success story is met with praise or celebration spearheaded by the leader and supported by the peers. When team members take pride in their work, there is no limit to what can be achieved.

In a 2015 article titled, "Why You Must Celebrate Small Successes", business technology specialist Minda Zetlin (co-author of "The Geek Gap"), writes that in order to succeed in a big endeavour, you must "parcel the journey out into the smaller steps you'll take along the way" and "celebrate when you reach each one."

Simple, creative ways of celebrating successes are opportunities to build the leader into a brand.

A leader should be on the lookout to "catch team members doing things right", and every opportunity should be celebrated in a creative way. The celebration need not be expensive. For most team members it is the thought or intention that counts.

Often, even the simple gift of a good quality ballpoint pen to any team member who achieves some success works wonders. The gift would be accompanied by a sincere comment such as "(Name), Congratulations on the job well done!" Or let the gift just be a chocolate bar for the successful team member's son or daughter with the words, "This is for your child, and tell her it is a gift from me to her for a good job done by her father / mother".

It bears repetition that it is the thought, timing, intent, and consistency that count in celebrating successes with your team members. Handwritten cards, saying "Congratulations" or "Thank you" on a job well done, will go a long way in building the 'brand' of leadership which celebrates success – in short, your leadership brand.

How do we celebrate successes that are unquantifiable, unlike sales numbers?

There are many such activities which team members do which may not be as visible as 'sales', nevertheless, these activities contribute positively and significantly to the culture of the company and build camaraderie in the workplace.

For example, in the absence of a team member, a colleague substitutes selflessly and meets a customer's demand in time. Such activities may not have a number attached to it, but no one can deny that it is a success story that needs to be shared and supported by the leader. Going the extra mile for a colleague will build a culture and a habit in the team to do one's part when some colleague is indisposed or fighting some other war.

Sharing best practices publicly opens the flood gates of positivity and learning. Usually, this is undertaken during mid-year or annual conferences, where the entire team meets with senior and global level executives. Employees who achieve breakthrough success are invited to present their success stories on this platform on certain parameters which is followed by a Q&A session, which is usually the highlight of the event. The presenter is flooded with critical questions, on how it was done, the method adopted, challenges overcome, and so on.

Such sessions serve as very practical and interactive learning forums where insights are dug up and it resonates with team members as they live the very same challenges day in and day out. Incidentally, such forums provide far better learnings than many training sessions on how to be successful.

Another method adopted is poster presentation (rather than boring PowerPoint presentations) of a success. This requires a lot of hard work as the presenter has to repeat the success story as many times as audience members turn up in front of the poster. A panel of judges assesses the best performances for felicitation.

The entire exercise works on the motto: **'Share passionately, copy intelligently'**. Such wide-angle and larger than life events celebrating employee successes are a worthwhile investment by the organization as it has a significant impact on the entire team aspiring to be in the elite club. The value of such showcasing far outstrips monetary compensation for an employee any day.

Parameters for the presenters:

- **The Objective:** Defining goals is the 1st step towards any big breakthrough
- **The Challenge:** In-depth understanding of the eco system before an action plan
- **The Action Plan:** Step by step progress detailing, leaving as little as possible to chance
- **The Innovation:** Yesterday's excellence, today's commonplace, tomorrow's obsolete
- **The Resources:** Deploying scarce resources to achieve success
- **The Collaboration:** Explaining how networks were leveraged
- **The Result:** Sharing results with others helps other also see possibilities
- **The Future of this project:** Good ideas get copied; ensure the customer stays with you

Exercise:

Imagine you were to present your latest success to an audience comprising your whole organization. Write your plan of action for each of the parameters given below:

The Objective: Defining the goals is the 1st step towards any big breakthrough.

The Challenge: In-depth understanding of the eco system before an action plan is made.

The Action Plan: Step by step progress detailing, leaving as little as possible to chance.

The Innovation: Yesterday's excellence, today's commonplace, tomorrow's obsolete.

The Resources: How scarce resources were deployed to achieve success.

____

____

____

____

____

____

The Collaboration: Explaining the leveraging of internal and external networks for success.

____

____

____

____

____

The Result: Sharing results with others helps others also see possibilities.

____

____

____

____

The Future of this Project: Good ideas get copied; did the customer stay with you or was poached by a competitor?

____

____

____

____

It is also important to note that all celebrations and recognitions must be offered for meaningful jobs done; where the leader can clearly or specifically articulate the reason for the celebration / recognition. 'Job well done', 'Great effort', 'Huge help to the team' — are incompletely articulated reasons for celebration. It leaves the recipient and the team members confused on what he or she has been complimented for! Even for intangible contributions, such as a team member stepping in for his or her indisposed colleague on an important client meeting must be translated into numbers (revenue generated, or what would have been the cost to the company of losing the client altogether).

The 10 Golden Keys to Successful Success Sharing:

1. Generating success on a frequent basis is the responsibility of the leader
2. The success needs to be meaningfully defined as per set standards
3. 'Catching them doing things right' generates desirable team and organizational culture
4. Large momentum is built when everyone wants to be caught doing things right
5. Success sharing creates a sense of community and the team members take pride in their work
6. The leader must ensure that the least member of the organization feels valued
7. Timeliness, authenticity, consistency, and right intent are vital elements of success sharing
8. 'No success is too small to share', as these are the building blocks towards the final goal
9. A leader's brand is built on his or her approach to celebrating successes with the team

10. Celebration in public and with personal recognition makes many aspire for success

Exercise:

Give some examples of you celebrating success of your team members.

____

____

____

____

____

____

Write a congratulatory note to a team member for a job well done.

____

____

____

____

____

____

Think of some innovative ways to celebrate success and build your 'brand' of leadership.

____

____

____

____

____

Have you missed any opportunity in the last three months to celebrate the success of your team members? If yes, Why? If no, what did you celebrate?

____

____

____

____

____

____

If yes, please list it so that it will not be overlooked in the future.

____

____

____

____

____

How would you like to develop your personal leadership brand in celebrating successes?

____

____

____

____

____

____

Key learnings from this chapter for you:

1.

2.

3.

4.

The Ritz-Carlton has a daily "Wow Story" session during the team huddle. A "Wow Story" is a verbal show-and-tell that illustrates an employee delivering an amazing guest experience or embodying Ritz Carlton's core cultural values. Sharing these stories reinforce three organizational outcomes:

- *Make important cultural values and brand promises clear, understandable, and relatable.*
- *Provide an inspiring and fun way to recognize and appreciate the greatness.*
- *Communicate "You matter. Your great work makes a difference."*

These wow stories do not have to be recorded and curated only by the HR team but by appreciative peers too. So it becomes a community enterprise. Leadership at the Ritz-Carlton has mastered the art of celebrating successes.

The 10 Golden Keys to Successful Success Sharing

Generating success on a frequent basis is the responsibility of the leader.

"Success" needs to be meaningfully defined and be as per set standards.

'Catch them doing things right'... it generates positive team and organizational culture.

A large momentum is built when everyone wants to be caught doing things right.

Success sharing creates a sense of community and the team members take pride in their work.

The leader must ensure that the least member of the organization feels valued.

Timeliness, authenticity, consistency, and right intent are vital elements of success sharing.

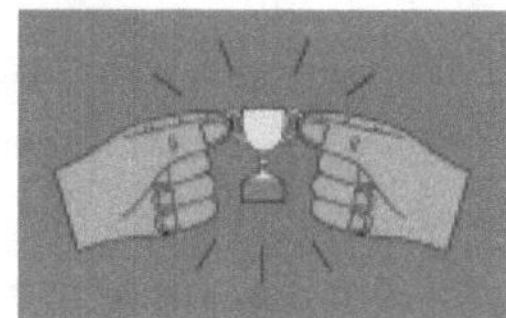

'No success is too small to share', as these are the building blocks towards the final goal.

A leader's brand is built on his or her approach to celebrating success with the team.

Celebration in public and with personal recognition makes many aspire for success.

LEADERSHIP ESSENTIAL # 9
INNOVATION

In 1891, William Wrigley started a soap business with baking powder offered as a freebie. However, the promotional baking powder became more popular than the soap and Wrigley shifted his focus. Now, he started selling baking powder with chewing gum as a promotional offer. Somehow the chewing gum became more popular than the baking powder. The innovative Wrigley shifted his focus again. Chewing gum thereafter became his new product and he launched Juicy Fruit and Wrigley's Spearmint. The rest, as they say, is history, 120 years in the writing.

Another innovation story is that of India's OYO Hotels. Frustrated with poor quality stay arrangements Ritesh Aggarwal created OYO Rooms, which has now become the world's third-largest and fastest-growing hospitality chain of leased and franchised hotels, homes & living spaces in just six years. Today Aggarwal's OYO is operating in Asia, Europe and the Americas. Success mantra: *innovative and disruptive business model.*

Innovation is flexible

Innovation is real. It is multidimensional. And it is difficult. Hence, moving with innovative ideas is no easy task. Innovators are also never stuck in their ways. They change directions as the situation demands.

Innovation is often the opposite of "flashes of brilliance" or "the big idea". Often it is seeded small, gradually gaining momentum and becoming disruptive. Twitter, for example, was the result of a new way of looking at the very nature of communication. In organizations, the acceptability of only fully proven ideas stifles innovation. Innovation is often incubated rather than planned. The appropriate ecosystem must be created for innovation to flourish.

Rosabeth Moss Kanter, Professor at Harvard Business School, states that innovation and leadership are affected by a leader's thinking process and behavioural preference.

THINKING PROCESS	BEHAVIOURAL REFERENCE
Analytical leaders – rigorous analysis, measures even small ideas	Expressiveness – understands full spectrum of team members' expressiveness from quiet to gregarious
Structural Leaders – practical; prepares guidelines and schedules	Assertiveness – knows when to push employees and when to step back on innovation
Conceptual Leaders – visionary, creative, imaginative; enjoys the unusual, encourages new techniques for innovation	Flexibility – decides on leader-led or crowdsourced innovation
Social Leaders – relational; focused on building right team environment for innovation	Perseverance – continues to forge ahead against obstacles

Exercise

What thinking process characterizes you as a leader in terms of innovation?

____

____

____

____

What is your behavioural preference while leading innovation? Do you wish to change it for better outcomes?

____

____

____

____

____

Innovation is not an Individual Level Activity

In a business setting it is a mistake to think of innovation as an individual-level activity. Business innovation is a collaborative effort starting from ideation through development to implementation involving multiple groups. An innovation focused leader must possess skills that make this collaboration possible. Collaboration helps others see the 'big picture' by coordinating rival groups, allocating resources, liaising with stakeholders, and by being encouraging in times of innovation failures.

From being an irregular ad hoc activity, effective leaders know that innovation is now on centre- stage in organizations. It drives growth, performance and valuation and is no longer a fad. According to a 2018 McKinsey report on Leadership and Innovation, innovation is seen by many top-level leaders as the most important way to accelerate the pace of change. Innovation has moved out of traditional product and service domains to processes, distribution, value chains, business models, and every other business sphere.

Innovation value creation is moving downstream

Much of customer grabbing innovation is happening downstream, according to Professor Niraj Dawar of Ivey Business School, Canada. What this means is that useful, profitable innovation is not about what you do inside your organization but what you do outside your organization for your customers. The locus of customer stickiness has moved outside. Innovative leaders, therefore, have to work with not only their own internal departments but also with downstream partners such as distributors, wholesalers, stockists, logistics partners, banking and financing partners, and so on.

Modern leaders have to think at multiple levels and perspectives. A career salesperson moving into a leadership role will have to think much wider than just innovative practices in acquiring and growing customers and driving numbers. He or she must now envision innovation across the board. As a leader, he or she must apply influence in all spheres of the business and its employees, as also vendors, bankers, media partners, and so on.

The skills set required to move from an executive manager to an innovative leader is not an incremental jump but an exponential leap. Most organizations do not offer a new incumbent the luxury of time to learn. It is assumed that learning will happen 'on-the-job'. Most leaders have been found unable to stimulate innovation at scale level where it can have a positive financial impact.

Time and again two factors have been identified as the biggest drivers of innovation – people and corporate culture. It is the responsibility of the leader to ensure that both people and the culture are innovation-conducive.

Exercise

What were the two things about your previous organization you found to be unsuitable for an innovative climate?

1.____

____

____

____

____

2.____

____

____

____

Do you think the innovativeness quotient of a leader has any impact on team members? Give one example either way.

____

____

____

____

____

____

____

____

____

____

____

As a leader when did you last encourage an innovative (defined as something not done at your organization before) initiative to improve business results? Describe the situation.

____

____

____

____

____

____

____

____

____

____

Did you notice any impact on your team members after the above initiative? If yes, what impact? If not, why not?

____

____

____

____

____

____

Two Components of Innovation Leadership

Innovation Leadership has two components – An innovative approach to leadership and leadership for innovation.

The first is about applying innovative thinking to leadership tasks. For instance, when unable to build a strong distribution network on its own, one automobile company tied up with another automobile brand. That is an innovative channel management leadership.

The second is about the organizational climate for innovation to happen. For instance, one software company is at the cutting edge of the market thanks to its employees coming up with a string of innovative product and process ideas. They ascribe the prolific idea generation to an organizational culture that encourages mistakes and false starts.

Two kinds of Managerial Thinking

The *Business Thinking* way is what most managers are adept at. It is based on facts, data, analysis, formula and logic. It focuses on removing ambiguity and quick decision making. It is based on past precedents. Managers are trained in business schools to operate in this ecosystem.

The *Innovative Thinking* way is what most managers are *not* adept at. It is intuitive and less based on facts. It focuses on embracing ambiguity and speed of decision making is secondary. It is not based on past precedents. Managers often do not have much training in innovating or building an innovative culture.

The Business Thinking Way	The Innovative Thinking Way
Logical	Intuitive
Dependent on past precedence	Open to multiple possibilities
Attempts to eliminate ambiguity	Embraces ambiguity
Quick decision making	Speed is of secondary importance
Trained in this way in formal education	May not be trained formally in this way

Exercise

Based on the above table, mark with an X where your personal 'thinking way' lies at present on the continuum below.

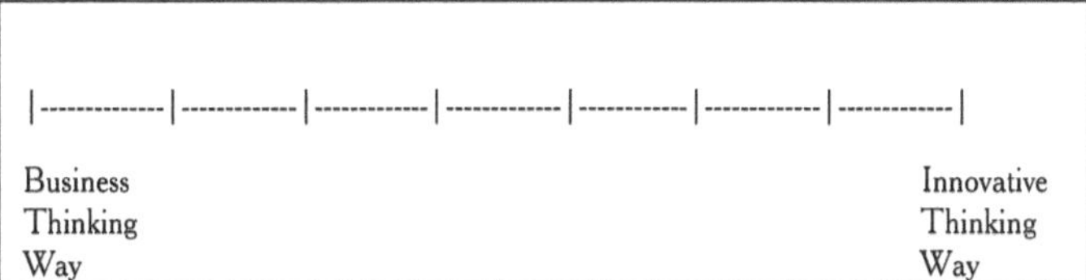

Skills to Up Your Innovative Thinking

Actively listen – Slow down, absorb the situation, don't jump to conclusions based on first appearances, develop the habit of looking beyond the obvious, search for nuances, hunt for details.

Value personal experience – Tap into personal life experiences. For instance, a football team manager who was once a player would be able to better coordinate the team members' different rates of absorbing new technology.

Visualize Information – It helps in processing a large amount of information and picturing the desired future. For instance, one might imagine a large number of people working in groups in a hall and the innovative solution coming from the fusion of the ideas of two groups in close proximity.

'Funnify' work – The most innovative ideas come from people at play, having fun, and enjoying themselves. Moments of serendipity crop up when least expected. Encourage fun at work, even in serious businesses such as consulting and education; scientific inquiry and plane

building. Rigidity kills creativity. Loosen up and let the creative juices flow.

Share Knowledge – Collate and create new information from the inputs of various stakeholders. For instance, a leading global technology company hires people from diverse fields such as music, mathematics, astronomy, geography and veterinary sciences. The result is innovation at a rapid pace to make it the world-beating internet search company it has become.

Synthesize Ideas – Have the ability to embrace two opposing ideas in your mind at the same time and yet function. It's about integrating and resolving contradictions. For instance, while prototyping a new product, can you function with two opposing ideas such as expensive, upmarket versus inexpensive, lower segment?

Exercise

In your role as an innovation leader, how do you self-evaluate on the following?

Active Listening:

Totally Me|------------|------------|------------|------------|Not Me at All

Visualizing Information:

Totally me|------------|------------|------------|------------|Not Me at All

Funnify Work:

Totally Me|------------|------------|------------|------------|Not Me at All

Share Knowledge:

Totally Me|------------|------------|------------|------------|Not Me at All

Synthesize Ideas:

Totally Me|------------|------------|------------|------------|Not Me at All

Key learnings from this chapter for you:

1.

2.

3.

4.

Pierre Omidyar and the auctioning website innovation. In 1995, a computer programmer started auctioning off stuff on his personal website. AuctionWeb, as it was then known, was just a personal project, but as web traffic grew it made it necessary to upgrade to a business internet account and Omidyar had to start charging a fee. Today that site is known as eBay. Innovative skills are sometimes unpredictable where they will take you. Leadership is a lot like entrepreneurship. You really don't know where you will end up. But being innovative is one critical factor in the success rate being higher for such leaders.

Matsushita innovates into electronic glory. In 1918 Japan, a 23-year-old apprentice Konosuke Matsushita at the Osaka Electric Light Company came up with an improved light socket. His boss wasn't excited about it. So young Matsushita started making samples in his basement. He later expanded to battery-powered bicycle lamps and other electronic products. Matsushita Electric, as it was known until 2008 when the company officially changed its name to Panasonic, is now worth $66 billion. Especially when nobody believes in what you are doing with your innovative skills is when one should try to stay innovative. In tough business times, leaders must find a way to be innovative to protect and grow the team and business.

Skills to improve Innovative Thinking
Actively Listen:
Absorb the situation, look beyond the obvious,
Hunt for details, don't jump to conclusions.
Visualize Information:
Process large amount
of information;
Picture the desired future.
Value Personal
Experience:
Tap into your own
personal life experiences
and those of others.
Experience teaches.
Funnify Work :
Encourage fun at work, Loosen up,
Let the creative juices flow.
Share Knowledge:
Integrate, Synthesize and
Resolve contradictions.

LEADERSHIP ESSENTIAL # 10
SITUATIONAL LEADERSHIP

Different strokes for different folks for different jobs.

What is the best leadership style?

If asked this question, what would your answer be?

Most leaders would reply, "It depends on the situation". But often we see people in charge of others using a singular style of leadership – *laissez-faire*, participative, democratic, or autocratic.

Let's consider the toolbox of a carpenter, it has multiple tools for different tasks — hammer, saw, chisel, wrenches, screwdrivers, pliers, planes etc. Each tool has a specific purpose. Using the right tool for a given job makes the desired outcome easier and faster to achieve. The carpenter will not use a hammer to cut a piece of wood or remove a nail.

There is a wise saying, 'If you only have a hammer then everything looks like a nail'.

So, a leader who has only one leadership style will use this one style in all situations and the results may not be too pleasant.

This is the very basis of situational leadership thinking: to adjust or customize your leadership style to the task and the person doing the task.

Let's discuss the background of Situational Leadership (SL) theory.

SL theory was developed by Paul Hersey and Kenneth Blanchard in 1969 as a leadership lifecycle framework. They state that there is no 'single best' form of leadership. What's 'best' would depend on various factors or situations. This primarily means that the leadership style to be used will be decided by the task to be performed and the level of competence and commitment level of the team member(s) performing that particular task.

The SL framework is a tool to help develop team members as they progress through their career life stages over a period of time so that they can reach the highest level of performance.

The SL framework asserts that there are many variables that a leader needs to take into account while dealing with people and thereafter consciously and purposefully select the leadership style that best suits a situation.

Every individual has his or her own dominant leadership style. However, using one leadership style across situations and people is inadvisable. Micro-managing your team might be resented by highly skilled or highly motivated team members in a routine job. Members with low skills might feel ignored if the leader does not hand-hold. The SL framework helps the leader to diagnose the situation and then choose the *optimal leadership style for that situation.*

The leader must, therefore, re-evaluate his or her own dominant leadership style on a regular basis and check for suitability at a given moment for a specified task.

Let's understand the diagram below:

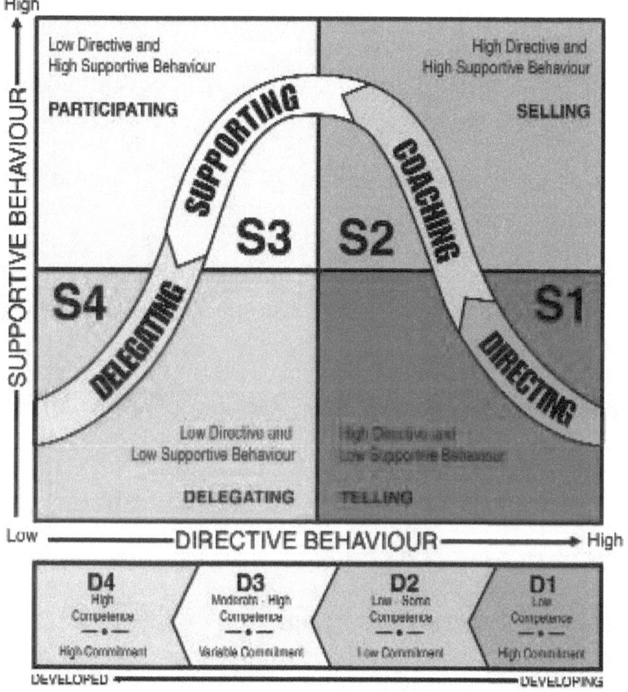

The 'X' axis represents Directive Behaviour (amount of direction that a leader gives a team). Higher the directive behaviour, less the team is allowed to make decisions for itself and less the dialogue between the leader and team members.

The 'Y' axis indicates supportive behaviour (encouragement and motivation a leader offers the team). Higher the support, more the team makes decisions on its own and more the dialogue and discussion between the leader and team members.

The bar at the bottom of the chart represents the development needs of the team members being led.

Development need is a factor of two parameters:

a) Commitment: Team member's motivation and confidence to take on a task.
b) Competence: Team member's skill or aptitude to complete the task.

The stages of development can be labelled by considering these two factors.

Going from right to left, the team member becomes more competent and more confident for a specific task. It indicates how well developed or motivated the team member is.

Here, D1 stands for the lowest level and D4 is the highest level of development.

D1 — Low competence but high commitment.

The enthusiastic beginner.

Typically, these are new employees or those new to a specific task, who lack experience but show enthusiasm to learn how to complete the task.

They lack specific skills to complete the task, but they are willing to learn and are excited by a new task.

At this stage, 'they don't know what they don't know'.

D2 — Some competence with low commitment

The disillusioned learner.

Here, the team member has some competence to complete the task but exhibits a lack of commitment (for whatever reason) to complete the task.

He or she might have faced some setbacks, failure or negative feedback, so commitment level is likely not as high as at the start. The task may also be proving to be tougher than what the expectation had been in the beginning.

The high excitement period is over at this stage and the initial enthusiasm wears off. The team member is probably confused now.

At this stage, the person is frustrated and may quit.

D3 — High competence with variable commitment.

The capable or cautious performer.

After a few months (time can differ with task and team member), the team member acquires the skills to do the task with less amount of supervision and completes the task as per the leader's expectation.

Here, the competence is more or less developed but the team member is yet to develop full confidence in terms of ability to repeat the task. Therefore, he or she approaches the task with caution.

At this stage, the individual is hesitant and unsure of how to repeat the task unsupervised.

D4 – High competence and high commitment.

The self-reliant achiever.

When a team member has demonstrated that he or she can deliver a task with a high level of competence and confidence over and over again, the leader decides to give this member more decision-making powers and he or she does work with little or no direction.

He or she trusts his or her own ability and is self-motivated.

At this stage, they are an inspiration to others.

In the following section, four different leadership styles suited for each development stage of members are discussed.

S1 — Directing: High directive and low supportive behaviour.

The leader makes all the decisions and the subordinate is not consulted. It is mostly one-way communication from the leader to the team member. The team member is expected to carry out instructions without any questions and feedback from the team is discouraged. The leader decides who, what, when, where and how. This is also known as the 'autocratic' type of leadership. Boss's favourite line: "My way or the highway".

Have you behaved in the "Directing" leadership style with anyone in your team? Why?

____

____

____

____

____

S2 — Coaching: High directive and high supportive behaviour.

Here, the leader takes feedback from the team member who is also encouraged to seek answers and clarify doubts. There are both one-way and two-way communications, but the leader still defines the roles and responsibilities for the task.

Leaders 'sell' their ideas and tasks to the team member(s) to get their cooperation. This leadership style is close to the 'democratic' style of leadership.

A good sports coach demonstrates this type of leadership. He puts the players in a field and then directs them as a team, together, for the benefit of the team's best performance.

Have you "Coached" anybody in your team? How?

____

____

____

____

____

S3 – Supporting: Low directive and high supportive behaviour.

The team member at this stage need not be told what needs to be done, although there is still some more development to be done. The leader will leave most of the decision making to the team members, although he or she may participate in the decision-making process as and when required. The leader seems like an equal team member as he or she participates with the other team members in idea generation and decision making.

In your business, how much time does a team member take to get to the stage where you can adopt a "Supporting" Leadership Style?

____

____

____

____

S4 – Delegating: Low directive and low supportive behaviour.

By this stage the team member is fully developed, so he or she can complete assigned tasks independently. This style of leadership is more 'hands-off', similar to *laissez-faire* (no interference) leadership, where the group makes more or less all the decisions and the leader provides the resources and the tools to complete the task.

Nevertheless, the leader is responsible for the performance of the team and continuously communicates the vision of the team or organization and the importance of getting the task completed as per pre-decided parameters.

Let us discuss a situation that most of us can relate to, but outside the work area.

Shaina has turned 18 and she has been waiting for this day when she can start driving a car.

She requests her father to teach her driving, to which he agrees.

Now visualize the first day she starts to learn driving with her father. She is full of enthusiasm and wants to learn fast so that she can get her driver's license quickly.

Her father gives directions and instructs her on the various functions and car parts, the accelerator, clutch, brake, gears, steering wheel, driving rules and regulations, and traffic signals symbols.

Shaina is a fast learner and memorizes everything and is back the next day for a hands-on training session with the driving instructor.

Her driving instructor tells her what she needs to do and she is asked to follow the instructions in totality, without any deviation.

She follows the directions and starts to implement what has been taught and coordinates between the clutch, accelerator, gears and steering.

The instructor gives her his full attention and keeps giving her specific directions. As she progresses, she asks questions on the task and her instructor answers them specifically and gets her back to the task.

She slowly understands the skills which improve over time under the direction of her instructor.

Before she started, driving seemed to be very easy as her friends and family members drove so effortlessly, chatting with the people in the car and listening to their favourite music. But with time, she gets to understand that it can be tiring and that she must be careful of other reckless drivers on the roads. The task, it seems, is not as simple as anticipated, and the initial enthusiasm wears off.

While driving, her coordination between the clutch, accelerator and gears sometimes slackens and the engine stops. This results in honking and shouting from the people driving behind her, and she gets jittery which leads to demotivation and frustration. Sometimes it reaches a point where she wants to give up on her driving (task).

Here, the instructor coaches her to accept that failure is part of the journey. He acknowledges and praises her progress at the opportune moments which slowly reinforce her desire to do the task and brings back her confidence and commitment.

With proper coaching, she becomes more competent to drive, but she still lacks full confidence.

Now her instructor helps her to make decisions on how to overcome the issues faced and encourages her to keep on overcoming challenges.

With time and practice, Shaina learns almost all the nuances of how to drive the car in various conditions and she becomes self-reliant. She can drive on her own and enjoy the freedom and have fun driving, but within the rules of the game and remembering her responsibility.

We must understand that the leadership style is 'situational' and is applicable in normal situations.

Suppose, a truck comes speeding from the wrong direction or the vehicle in front of her brakes suddenly. This is an emergency situation. Her instructor can give directions on what is to be done, or he may himself pull the hand brake. There would not be any time to coach or support or delegate the task to Shaina.

<u>Exercise</u>

- Discuss a task that you had given to the team in the recent past and plot the development needs and the leadership style you had adopted for each of your direct reports.

Team Member	Task	Development Level	Leadership Style Adopted	Was the adopted leadership style effective? If not, what would you do differently?

A	Ex: Get the newly launched drug into the prescription list of 20 key doctors in 30 days	D2: Development Level: Low; Competence: moderate; Motivation: Low	Directing; clear instructions given; regular monitoring performed	Yes. It was the only effective option as members had moderate competence and low motivation level
B				
C				

By now it must be clear that effective leaders adjust their leadership style on broadly three parameters:

1. The task that needs to be completed
2. The maturity level or competencies of the team member(s) for the task
3. The motivation level of the team member(s) to take on the task.

Customized leadership styles which can adapt to any situation and employee competence-motivation level is the only way to achieve great results from a team of people with varying competencies and commitment

How do you develop high-quality situational leadership skills? The answer lies in nurturing the following:

1. Flexibility and versatility
2. Deep understanding of the team, especially competence and motivators
3. Leader's own self-awareness level
4. Clarity of the task at hand with distinct time-bound goals (SMART Goals)

Let's discuss the above points now.

Flexibility and Versatility

Flexibility is an important requirement in situation leadership. It requires maturity and an open mind and demands alertness to every team member's specific requirements. However, it can also be perceived as unfair by some team members – you are 'supportive' of one team member and 'directing' with another. Hence, the team members should also be apprised of the need for each style being adopted for different team members.

Situational leadership is a continuous process. It is not about changing one's leadership style once in a while but on a need basis whenever the situation warrants it. This calls for knowing and applying different leadership styles in different situations. This needs versatility, the ability to use different methods and taking on different roles.

Things to be aware of:

1. Different team members might misunderstand your different styles for different folks.
2. Team members need to be educated on a one-on-one basis of leadership style differences.
3. Organizational culture plays an important part in one's flexibility and versatility.
4. It is not a one-off thing; it must become an integral part of one's professional interactions

Deep understanding of the team.

Having a deep understanding of the team members' personal, social and professional background as well as their behavioural aspects (how they respond to crises, what motivates them, cultural background, how they work in teams) will help determine the leadership style that needs to be adopted for a specific task.

Leadership is about developing the team and it requires chalking out a development plan for each member. Therefore, understanding the team members will be beneficial to the entire organization, as each and every team member can be developed to the next level as the leader provides the right development tools and methods.

Things to be cautious of:

1. Shallow knowledge of the team member's nature, social needs and skillsets will result in inappropriate use of a particular leadership style.
2. Inappropriate use of leadership style will not get the desired result and worse may induce conflict or dissatisfaction amongst team members.
3. It would be suboptimal to consider a team member only as a resource person; reach deeper.

High self-awareness.

Self-awareness is an important aspect of leadership, and we have dedicated a complete chapter to it (Chapter 2 of this Leadership Essentials workbook).

Self-awareness becomes so much more relevant in situational leadership, as one needs to not only be aware of one's own natural leadership style but also learn to apply the leadership style which is best suited for the situation.

A question might come to your mind, "Instead of the leader changing his style as per the needs of the team members, should it not be the other way around?" Should team members not adjust their style of doing things to the leader's style of leadership? The answer is 'no'. For better performance outcomes, it is easier for the leader (one person) to change his or her style than the team members (many).

The relationship between the leader and the team member(s) will determine the performance readiness of the team member(s) to approach a task. Based on the above relationship, when the appropriate leadership style is applied, the right blend of task behaviour and relationship behaviour will ensure the right outcome. Self-awareness will determine how much relationship equity the leader enjoys with the team.

Things to be cautious of:

1. Self-awareness is not as simple as it sounds. It needs a proper process of reflection best done with a professional coach.
2. The full awareness of the self can often be traumatic for many individuals. One must prepare mentally before attempting a full disclosure of one's true self.
3. Once mastered, self-awareness can elevate leadership effectiveness tremendously.

Clarity of the task at hand with distinct time-bound goals (SMART Goals)

Leadership is about reaching a goal successfully by team members.

Hence, the task has to be well defined with clear roles and responsibilities, only then will the leader be able to customize his or her leadership style.

Vague tasks and directions lead to disenchantment; motivated members gradually slack off as they hardly know what is expected of them.

We have discussed SMART goals in an earlier chapter, which is the *mantra* for any effective goal setting activity.

Situational leaders, or any leader for that matter, should communicate tasks based on the SMART parameters. This will not only clarify the roles and responsibilities but also make the team take ownership of the task at hand.

The right match between a role, development level (competencies / skill) and motivation (willingness to do the task) is the critical judgment that the leader makes. A situational leader will work keeping these three elements in mind while deciding the leadership style that needs to be adopted.

Raj is the leader of an FMCG sales team. Let's discuss the tasks of his various team members.

The task at hand is to develop business from 3 new retail chains. The SMART objective: To get business entry into three retail chains —Sunlight Retail, Moonlight Retail and Starlight Retail in the next quarter and generate business of Rs. 500,000 from each within the next six months. All documentation, proposal submission including quotations and the first meeting with key stakeholders are to be completed within 45 days.

Jenny, Anil, Iqbal & Sunil are Raj's four team members.

Jenny has just joined the company and has high enthusiasm and works hard to understand the job but lacks skills for the task at hand. This particular task is very new to her but she is willing to put in extra hours to equip herself for the job.

Anil has been with the company for the last six years and has delivered on his task with great enthusiasm and has upskilled himself to deliver performance above expectations and still exhibits these qualities in any new assignment. His skill level is quite high for this type of task so is his willingness to do the task.

Iqbal is the longest-serving member in Raj's team, 10 years to be exact. He has delivered on projects in the past with a great deal of enthusiasm and dedication. His skill level for this task used to be good in the past. Now it is variable, sometimes he does a good job, at other times poor quality work. His motivation to take up new tasks has been decreasing steadily and is at a low level at present.

Sunil has been with the company for more than a year. He has not delivered yet on his commitment for this type of task as he lacks the required skills. Further, he has also not exhibited enthusiasm to upgrade himself. His energy levels are quite low.

Now allocate the above team members in the below Skill–Will matrix.

The Skill-Will Matrix is derived from the model of situational leadership created by Paul Hersey and Ken Blanchard.

In this model, the employee's performance of a task is related to two parameters:

a)   Skill — his or her capability to do that task.
b)   Will — his or her commitment and motivation to approach and complete that task.

The leadership style will depend on which quadrant the team member is in.

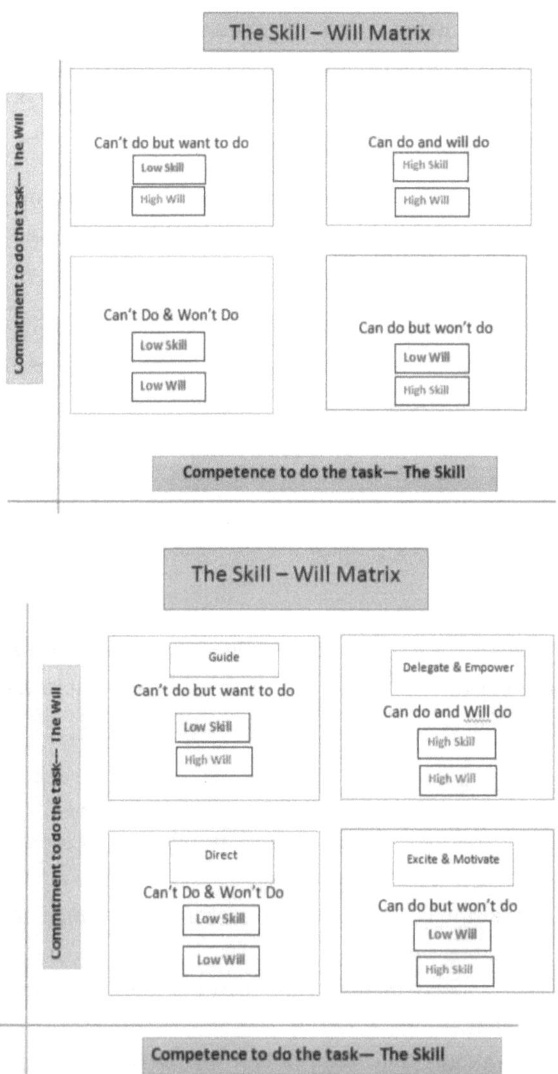

Should Raj use the same leadership style to manage all four of his team members for this task?

The answer is 'no'.

It would be such a waste of executive time. It would also possibly cause some amount of resentment amongst some of the team members if an inappropriate leadership style is applied to any of the team members.

Each team member has different needs and different ways to be managed for a particular task. This is the basis of situational leadership.

Let us take each situation and discuss the leadership style that is the most appropriate and work on the steps to be followed by the leader to maximize outcomes.

High Skill & Low Will (HSLW)

The team member used to be a good performer in the past for this particular task, and has the required skills, but lacks the will of late.

He or she may have got bored due to the repetitiveness of the job. Frustration could be due to past good efforts having gone unnoticed and unrewarded.

Steps to be followed:

1. Have an open discussion and find the reason for current demotivation for the task.
2. Explain why the member's contribution is important to the team's progress.
3. Find aspects of the task which can motivate the team member.
4. Give adequate praise publicly for the progress made.

Suggested leadership style to be adopted here: 'Excite & Motivate' a 'high skill-low will' team member. Raj needs to *'Excite & Motivate'* Iqbal.

High Skill & High Will (HSHW)

This team member is highly ambitious and wants to grow in the job. He is in the high-performance zone and is making rapid progress.

Steps to be followed:

1. Provide proper resources and give freedom to such members.
2. Seek their opinion and involve them in decision making.
3. Encourage the team member to take up more responsibilities.
4. Praise and reward success.

The leadership style here should be to 'Empower' the 'high skill-high will' team member. In order to get the best out of him, Raj's leadership style with Anil should be to *Empower* him.

Low Skill & High Will (LWHW)

These team members are usually new to the task and want to establish themselves in the eyes of their peers and superiors. They are enthusiastic to do the task and learn new skills which they currently lack.

Steps to be followed:

1. Create a learning environment and teach/ demonstrate specific skills for the job.
2. Ask to repeat instructions to confirm understanding.
3. Demonstrate how it is to be done and encourage execution under your supervision.
4. Give frequent feedback and praise progress.
5. Praise and reward success.

The leadership style appropriate for this type is to 'Guide' the team member. Hence, Raj needs to *Guide* Jenny to complete the task as explained above.

Low Skill & Low Will (LSLW)

'Low Skill-Low Will' team members come into play because:

i) They may have been assigned the wrong task against their will

ii) Are quite new to the task/team/organization and lack both confidence and skill

The leader needs to understand the team and explore the reasons why they fall in this category.

Steps to be followed:

1. Discuss and identify what will motivate the team member.
2. Build motivation before trying to upskill the member.
3. Demonstrate, provide resources and supervise on the job.
4. Set clear expectations and communicate what success looks like.
5. Offer regular feedback and praise progress.
6. Praise and reward success.

The leadership style to be adopted for 'low skill-low will' team members is to 'Direct'. Hence, Raj needs to *Direct* Sunil to get the best out him to complete the task.

We reiterate that situational leadership methods are 'task' based.

Suppose the company wants to introduce a new e-reporting platform, and Jenny happens to be very tech-savvy. So Raj will be using the 'empower' style of leadership for her.

Exercise:

Discuss two tasks that you expect two of your team members (the longest-serving – Member X; and the newest in your team – Member Y) to do in the next one month.

Place each of them in the appropriate quadrant on the Skill-Will matrix for this particular task.

Task for Member X:

____

____

____

Task for Member Y:

____

____

____

Mention the leadership style you would like to adopt for each of these two team members. Explain why.

____

____

____

____

____

____

____

____

____

____

Key learnings from this chapter for you:

1.

2.

3.

4.

Different strokes for Different folks – the Essence of Situational Leadership

14 students from elementary school to high school stood proudly on stage on the first day of the new school year. Their audience? 700 educational facilitators and leaders representing the ten campuses comprising a school district in Texas, USA.

One by one, the students shared personal examples of the challenges they faced every day dealing with dyslexia:

- "I can't speak as fast as my mind moves."
- "People don't understand me."
- "I'm not stupid, I have dyslexia."

Finally, one elementary school student summarized all the challenges:

"Don't grade me on my spelling, grade me on what I wrote about."

The impact of these messages was immediate and profound. There wasn't a dry eye in the house and it got everyone thinking about their flexibility — or lack thereof — as leaders of their respective schools or classrooms.

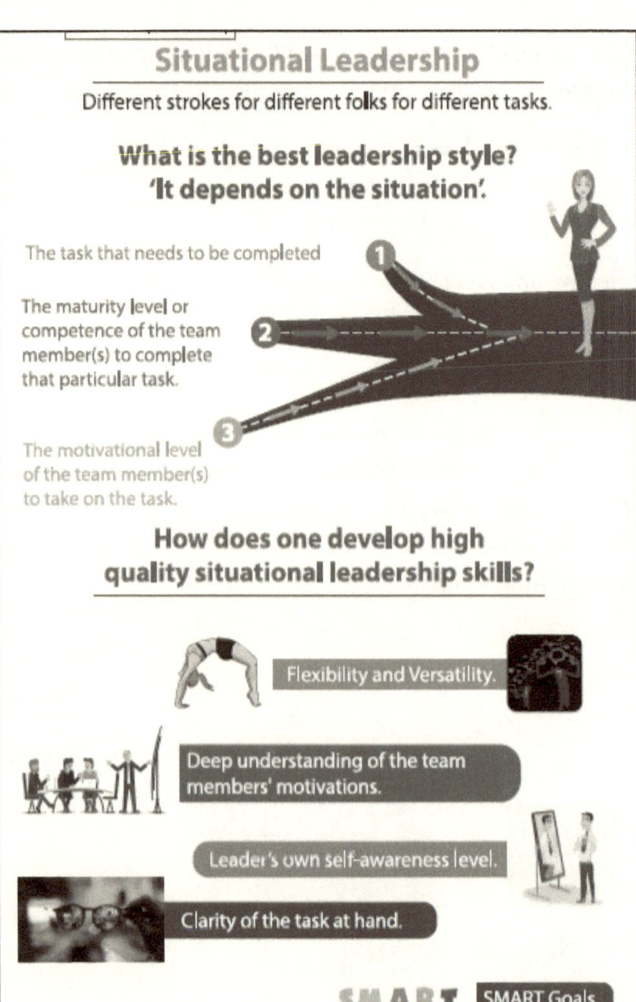

Situational Leadership
Different strokes for different folks for different tasks.
What is the best leadership style?
'It depends on the situation'.
The task that needs to be completed
1
The maturity level or competence of the team member(s) to complete that particular task.
2
3
The motivational level of the team member(s) to take on the task.
How does one develop high quality situational leadership skills?
Flexibility and Versatility.
Deep understanding of the team members' motivations.
Leader's own self-awareness level.
Clarity of the task at hand.
S.M.A.R.T
SMART Goals.

Epilogue – The Unique Leader

In your corporate career, you are likely to have already worked with (or are likely to work with in the future) a wide variety of leaders. Over time it will become clear that the personalities, styles and attitudes of leaders begin to repeat. Soon, leaders and leadership styles become predictable.

The most memorable leaders are those who are genuinely unique. They have a presence about them that helps them stand apart in a crowd. Their way of looking at things is "out of the box" and "unconventional". They may admire other leaders and learn from them too but they will never follow them mindlessly. Not only are their business decisions unique but so are the ways in which they support you in their personal capacity. They have your back and will stand up for you when times get tough. They sponsor you at work and help give you a platform to get discovered and propel your career forward.

You know that your leader is unique when he or she consistently goes out of his or her way to make you know that you matter. They are wise enough to attempt leveraging a skill or competency that other leaders did not notice or neglected in you. These leaders are characterized by deep self-awareness and self-trust, deep enough to appreciate the differences in others.

The Need For Uniqueness (NFU) is a trait in people that makes them seek differentness from others. High powered leaders might be very effective in business but not memorable enough as having stood up for a just cause or for having given a member of their team the personal touch in times of anguish or failure. High need for unique leaders set themselves clearly apart from other leaders in terms of both business acumen and personal approach. They are often remembered long beyond the tenure they serve in organizations. They live on in the hearts and minds of people. They leave behind a legacy of high profits and solid people.

As an aspiring leader, it would be worth seeking out a special place among the ones who lead. Examining your uniqueness quotient and pursuing the desire to stand apart from others would help you leave behind the sea of mediocrity and forge ahead as a unique leader.

Here finishes the first part of our leadership journey together. We hope it has been an enriching one. Do not be discouraged if all the insights and approaches shared here do not always come true for you in your leadership journey. The important thing is to set yourself on this odyssey and stay the course. Learn and act upon what has been provided to you in this workbook and add your own deep insights from time to time. Let us know too how to make this work richer and more useful for aspiring leaders like yourself.

Many thanks for picking up this book and choosing to act upon it! We sincerely hope that this book can be your companion in the pursuit of leadership excellence.

Partha Pratim Pal and Jones Mathew

AUTHOR PROFILES

Partha Pratim Pal

Partha is a veteran in the field of sales and marketing with more than 30 years of work experience in the highly competitive and regulated pharma industry.

A science graduate, Partha has been trained at Indian Institute of Management, Ahmedabad and holds an MBA in marketing.

In his three-decades-long corporate career, Partha has built multiple teams with a strong ethical and business orientation. His journey has also seen him mentor numerous young professionals who are leaders in the industry today. His expertise comes from his ability to learn from the mistakes made and successes achieved while pursuing high stakes assignments using innovative business strategies and employing situational leadership styles.

Partha's professional career has been one filled with national and international exposure. His work experience with major national and international pharmaceutical companies such as Ranbaxy, Zydus, and Allergan India, where he had the opportunity to lead the India & South Asia operations for its Neurosciences division. Leading teams across these geographies and the opportunity to work in complex market conditions gave him valuable insights into business and leadership.

A highly driven leader, Partha is passionate about training and mentoring the next generation of leaders in the industry, and to disseminate his learnings to future business leaders.

Jones Mathew

A PhD from the Indian Institute of Foreign Trade, New Delhi, Dr. Mathew has 30 years of work experience, of which 18 years were spent in Indian and multinational companies such as HCL Ltd, MECON, Yonex, and Reebok. His last held corporate position was of VP (Sales & Marketing) at an Indo-US joint venture.

Sales, Product and Brand Management, Vendor Development, Retail Operations and Marketing were his core areas in the corporate domain. He has been in academics for the last ten years and teaches Marketing Management, Product and Brand Management and Services Marketing to postgraduate students and working executives.

As a corporate trainer, Dr. Mathew has conducted Executive Development Programs (EDPs) for Nokia Siemens Networks, PHDCCI, IIFT, Women and Child Welfare Department, Govt of Delhi, and Somany Ceramics, among others.

He has authored research articles in international journals, popular press articles in the top Indian media outlets, and published case studies with Harvard Publishing, Ivey Publishing (Canada), and ECCH (Europe). He is the recipient of the 2016 ISB-Ivey Global Case Competition Marketing Category Winner award. Dr. Mathew is also on the advisory board of academic journals and is a member of the Research Development Council of three universities. At Great Lakes Institute of Management, Gurgaon, Dr. Mathew heads the Marketing Area, Rankings and Accreditations, and Research.

ABOUT THE BOOK

"The Leadership Essentials" is a *Workplace Series* presentation. The Workplace Series will focus on various aspects of success in the corporate domain. The Leadership Essentials is a collection of important action areas for succeeding in the most critical of business functions – leadership. The book is the distilled wisdom of the authors' combined professional experience in the pharmaceutical, lifestyle, sports and education domains. Leadership has many facets and many pitfalls. The important focus areas for successful leadership have been highlighted with examples. Divided into 10 chapters, the reader is taken through a set of workbooks to introspect, examine and position oneself for leadership roles.

The chapter themes have been developed and curated carefully so that the aspiring leader can maximize the benefits in an easy-going, conversational, step by step leadership journey. In every chapter, there are exercises to help the reader to practice and synthesize the lessons. This work focuses on 'Learning by Doing' as the most effective self-improvement technique. Whether it is SMART goal setting, vision development or situational leadership, this workbook has it all. Interesting vignettes add a unique flavor of relevance to each chapter. This book is intended to be an aspiring leader's constant companion. Existing leaders too can benefit from this book by reflecting upon and examining their leadership journey against the chapters here.